D1709147

SURVIVING ZOMBIE WARFARE

TIPS FOR YOUR ROAD TRIP THROUGH A
ZOMBIE WAR ZONE

SEAN T. PAGE

Cataloging-in-Publication Data

Names: Page, Sean T.
Title: Tips for your road trip through a zombie warzone / Sean T. Page.
   Description: New York : Rosen YA, 2019. | Series: Surviving zombie warfare |
Includes glossary and index.Identifiers: ISBN 9781508186434 (pbk.)
| ISBN 9781508186458 (library bound)
Subjects: LCSH: Zombies—Juvenile literature. | Survival—Juvenile literature.
| Travel—Miscellanea—Juvenile literature.
Classification: LCC PN6231.Z65 P345 2019 | DDC 818'.602—dc23

Manufactured in the United States of America

Originally published in English by Haynes Publishing under the title: *Zombie
Survival Transport Manual* © Sean T. Page 2017.

AUTHOR'S ACKNOWLEDGEMENTS

There were many experts involved in this book and I would
like to particularly thank Steve "Rusty" Langdon for answering
endless questions about his wasteland scooter and his war
stories. To Mrs Eileen Cassidy, for travelling to London on several
occasions and for allowing us to print plans to her apocalypse
shopping trolley. To Toyota, Honda, Hyundai and the RAC, who
provided some of the motoring inspiration for this volume. To
all the survivors who kindly contributed their vehicle plans and
case studies for inclusion – we couldn't fit them all in but they all
proved to be invaluable to our research. Finally, to my partners
in crime – Ian, Louise, and Richard – for their belief that such a
book is essential to help protect the country and for settling the
regrettable incident with the flame thrower out of court. Above
all, to my wife Constance and daughter Nikita, who is currently
converting her trike into a devastating wasteland cruiser.

 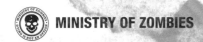

CONTENTS

GETTING AROUND IN ZOMBIELAND

In this manual, we interpret "transport" in the widest possible terms – that's why you'll find detailed schematics of many different forms of transport to carry you and your supplies, from pimped disability scooters all the way up to purpose-designed apocalypse campervans and even ultra light aircrafts.

In reality, most zombie preppers have a mix of vehicles depending on their requirements and it is important to consider your own "end of the world" needs before we delve into the mechanical detail. For example, we are going to assume that you already have a Bug-Out Plan – that is an emergency set of procedures to get you through the zombie apocalypse. Although there are thousands of variants of Bug-Out Plans, they generally fall into one of two categories and the zombie survival community is split over which is best. In the end, it comes down to a personal decision based on your own circumstances.

1) STAYING PUT

Broadly speaking, this means staying either at home or in a nearby location, fortifying it and seeing out the early chaos of the zombie apocalypse by staying off the streets. Typically, preppers opting for this survival strategy will use the Ministry of Zombies 90-Day Survival Plan which involves having 90 days worth of food, water, and supplies – the logic being that by sealing yourself and your family off you can escape the violent early phase of an outbreak when desperate survivors and growing numbers of the dead will be trawling our towns and cities for victims.

▶ TYPES OF VEHICLES

KEY FEATURES
BUG-OUT VEHICLE

- ▶ Built for extensive road trips
- ▶ Long-range capability (typically in excess of 400 miles on one tank)
- ▶ Mainly defensive armaments
- ▶ Good storage space for long-term bug-out supplies
- ▶ Room for the whole crew – could be used as living quarters
- ▶ Reinforced frontal grill and bull bars to enable the ramming of blocking vehicles
- ▶ Your vehicle will need off-road capability as apocalypse conditions are rarely perfect.
- ▶ Blends in. A vehicle stacked with supplies on the roof could be a tempting target.

"I'VE SEEN WHAT HAPPENS TO AN URBAN ENVIRONMENT DURING A ZOMBIE OUTBREAK IN SERBIA. THERE'S A LOT OF TALK ABOUT 'THE OFF-THE-ROAD WINDOW' AND KEEPING YOUR HEAD DOWN. IN REALITY, IT DOESN'T WORK. TO SURVIVE, YOU NEED A WELL-MAINTAINED BUG-OUT VEHICLE TO GET YOU TO SAFE LOCATIONS."
MICK 'FROSTY' HILLS, ZOMBIE SURVIVALIST, EX-SAS TROOPER

2) BUGGING-OUT

A phrase popular in the survival community, it refers to getting all of your family or team and supplies into a vehicle and getting the hell out of Dodge. Preppers preferring this strategy will have an agreed Bug-Out location and a detailed plan of how to get there, be it an off-shore island, an isolated farm or perhaps a large forest. The key factor in bugging-out is how to survive and complete the journey.

▶ The zombie survival community is split down the middle on the subject of staying put or bugging out. You'll find expert sources on the web extolling the virtues of both approaches.

▶ In a recent poll on a zombie survival forum, just over 53% favored staying in or close to home and this has been the survival orthodoxy for the last few decades.

▶ At the end of the day, a quality vehicle could perform both roles if required.

STAY PUT OR BUG-OUT?

In truth, many preppers mix and match these strategies – they may have a 90-Day Survival Plan set up around the house and also keep a Bug-Out Vehicle (sometimes known as a BOV) close by in case things turn frosty.

Equally, however, from a secure location, you may decide that embarking on a long journey at the height of the crisis is madness and that you only need a Zombie Apocalypse Vehicle (often known as a ZAV) for local foraging and raiding.

It's important not to get too bogged down in the difference between a BOV and a ZAV as to some extent it doesn't make that much difference. What is key is that you develop your transport solutions around your own zombie survival plan. If you plan to stay put then think about a light vehicle for raiding local sites. If you already have an agreed long-term survival location then you need something robust and big enough to get you and your party there, although that's not as simple as it sounds.

KEY FEATURES
ZOMBIE APOCALYPSE VEHICLE

▶ Short to medium range cruiser
▶ Able to hand most road conditions
▶ Designed for combat, with both defense and offensive weapons
▶ Storage space for foraged resources
▶ Well-able to handle any raiders in terms of speed and performance
▶ Could be a standard family car which is adapted once the dead rise
▶ Ensure you have a good stock of consumables and spares
▶ If you have the space and budget, an off-road motorcycle is an ideal secondary ZAV
▶ Remember to keep your vehicle safe during the first weeks of chaos.

"PEOPLE GET HUNG UP ON ALL THE ZOMBIE SURVIVAL TERMS. FORGET BOVS & ZAVS – IF YOU LIVE IN A TOWN OR CITY THE BEST POLICY IS TO STAY PUT AND GET THE RIGHT VEHICLE MIX TO DO THIS. THINK POWERFUL ROAD CRUISER FOR SERIOUS FORAGING AND DEALING WITH BANDITS."
JACK FALLOW, URBAN SURVIVORS FORUM

GETTING AROUND IN ZOMBIELAND

ASSESSING YOUR REQUIREMENTS

Before reading any further or putting a deposit down on an ex-US military Hummer you found on eBay, you should complete a transport needs assessment. For example, if your strategy is to stay put in a well-fortified home for the first 90 days before emerging to forage and loot in the wasteland, then a hardcore battle car might do the job, along with a good stock of fuel and spare parts – ideal for short-range raiding and scaring off the local gangs.

However, if stage one of your plan is to 'head out to the country' then you are going to need a suitable long-distance transport solution – like a bus. Basically, you'll need the capacity to transport you, your group and its supplies across some of the toughest environments. Ensure you consider the size, mix and ability of your party. Will they all be in one location? Review your Bug-Out Route – does it avoid built up areas?

In a survey by *Automotive* magazine, more than 90% of current road users were shown to be poorly prepared and equipped for motoring in the wake of a major zombie outbreak. That's a shocking statistic considering the ongoing work of organizations such as the Ministry of Zombies and the increasing popularity of zombie fiction and television shows. In most cases drivers just failed to grasp the gravity of the end of civilization – including an associated collapse in law and order.

> **"IF YOU'RE LOOKING AT HOW TO GET AROUND ONCE THE DEAD RISE, YOU CAN'T AFFORD TO IGNORE WHAT WILL BE GOING ON AROUND YOU. YOU'LL BE FACING THE CHAOS OF A MAJOR VIRAL OUTBREAK, WITH ALL THE DANGERS THAT WILL BRING. SO, THINK IT THROUGH AND PLAN CAREFULLY."**
> **KYE ANDERSON, FOUNDER OF ENDOFDAYS.COM AND EXPERT ZOMBIE PREPPER**

GETTING AROUND IN ZOMBIELAND
IMMEDIATE TRAVEL PLANS

It is interesting to note that, in transportation terms, very few in this country are prepared for the zombie apocalypse but just how unprepared are we as a nation? In April 2017, *Automotive* magazine carried out a survey of its readers to find out. They asked, "The country has been overrun by zombies, what are your immediate travel plans?"

48% **NONE – I'M KEEPING OFF THE ROADS**
"I've got a bunch of DVD box sets to binge on."

6% **CAUTIOUS BUT PREPARED**
"I've got my own plans, that's all you need to know."

9% **LOOTING**
"I'm planning to hit the local shopping center as soon as the dead rise – parking shouldn't be an issue."

13% **JUST LOCAL TRAVEL**
"I'll be using the first few days to check in on friends and neighbors; I might also do a bit of pillaging."

24% **PACK UP AND HIT THE ROAD**
"The wife and I have a delightful cottage down in the country. It's bound to be safe there."

SURVEY FROM *AUTOMOTIVE* MAGAZINE, APRIL 2016, 7,868 RESPONDENTS

MINISTRY OF ZOMBIES

Z-DAY

Z-Day is a nominal date zombie survivalists use to tag a particular date when the zombie hordes are in the ascendency. It's a concept used in planning. In reality, there won't be an official Z-Day. Things will start falling apart well before this date. Expect public transport to become sporadic and unreliable. Correction – expect public transport to become even more sporadic and unreliable. Think crowded buses but with the added spice of zombies. As has been the case in previous emergencies, it's less to do with breakdowns and traffic but more to do with drivers and other support staff not turning up.

The first 48 hours of a real zombie outbreak emergency will be the most dangerous. If your mint-condition anti-zombie cruiser is sitting on the drive – this is likely the time it will be stolen, looted, or destroyed beyond repair by desperate neighbors.

In reality, Z-Day will be a confusing period of weeks, a window when there is still a chance that the authorities will contain the outbreak. You won't be able to trust media reports so it's essential you have your own emergency protocols in place. For example, do you Bug-Out or go into lockdown at the first sign of cannibalism in the street? This is a decision you will need to make as a zombie prepper and there are plenty of resources available online to support the development of your own warning system.

THE OFF-THE-ROAD WINDOW

The first few months of a zombie outbreak are often referred to in zombie survival planning circles as the "Off-the-Road Window." This term is most relevant for urban survivors and is based on the assumption that the initial chaos and lawlessness of the opening months of any crisis is the ideal time to be hunkered down. Let the unprepared, the newly undead and the crazies battle it out on the street before emerging from your fortified bastion. Keep yourself and your vehicle secure and under wraps.

KEY EVENTS

▶ With your zombie outbreak monitoring systems in place, the moment you suspect a major incident, you need to enact your Bug-Out or Lock-Down Plans. Basically, get to where you need to be quickly before the chaos develops.

▶ Survival psychologists often talk about a 'period of denial' – a time when most of the populace will simply try to carry on as normal despite the growing madness. You'll hear talk of the authorities 'getting on top of the problem' or 'the government is sending a force'. Even if it's true, you can't take that chance. Your main advantage is knowledge so use it and act quickly.

▶ If you are locking down, try to keep a low profile. You may have the chance to top up on any last minutes supplies but be discreet – don't start a panic by dashing through the supermarket warning about the end of the world.

▶ Finally, once you are where you want to be, whether a Bug-Out Location or your fortified home, run silent and observe. Maybe the authorities will win back control, maybe the off-the-road window will last for months. You need to prepared for every scenario. Be adaptable, be alert and ready to act.

"THE IMMEDIATE AFTERMATH OF A ZOMBIE OUTBREAK IS NOT THE TIME TO BE STOCKING UP ON SUPPLIES AND CRUISING THE STREETS. THOSE OF US PREPARED FOR THE END MUST BE ON GUARD DURING THIS TIME. LET YOUR POST-APOCALYPTIC MOTORING BEGIN ONCE THOSE UNPREPARED HAVE BEEN CLEARED FROM OUR ROADS."
LORD ROSE, CHAIRMAN,
THE POST-APOCALYPTIC MOTORING ASSOCIATION

GETTING AROUND IN ZOMBIELAND

ASSESSING THE ZOMBIE CAPABILITIES

What about the dead themselves? Much of this manual is about preparing your transport options and plans for these end times so it's important you fully grasp the capabilities of these desperate and deadly creatures.

WHY FEAR THE WALKING DEAD?

A valid question asked by many new to zombie prepping. Many think that they might as well focus on their plans to battle bandits and human opponents, for example. However, although Zombies cannot use mass forms of transport, go for a Sunday drive or sign a hire-purchase agreement on a new Hyundai, they can get trapped under cars or buses, be swept along rivers with the current or wash up on beaches after drifting for weeks – in fact, they can travel many hundreds, even thousands, of miles. This is something to take into account in your zombie preparedness planning, but what about 'normal' zombie walking? We know they are relentless but how far could zombies realistically walk?

Quick answer – we don't know. For example, if you bugged out in your pimped post-apocalyptic vehicle to the very north of Maine, would the undead hordes of New York, Pennsylvania, or even Florida eventually follow you?

What we do have is zombie scientist and walking dead egg-head Dr Raymond Carter's latest thinking on a biological model for zombie movement – a 500 page rip-roaring geek read. Here is the key message:

"WE DO NOT YET FULLY UNDERSTAND THE CHEMICAL REACTIONS TAKING PLACE WITHIN THOSE WITH THE ZOMBIC CONDITION BUT WE CAN ASSUME THAT A STANDARD ENERGY EQUATION IS AT WORK. THUS, ZOMBIES DO HAVE A FINITE ENERGY RESOURCE WHICH EXPLAINS WHY MANY CREATURES SIMPLY FALL INTO DORMANT STATES WHEN NOT AROUSED BY THE PROSPECT OF LIVING HUMAN MEAT."
DR RAYMOND CARTER

GETTING AROUND IN ZOMBIELAND
FACTS ABOUT ZOMBIES

▶ Zombies are real. They are scientific fact, with hundreds of sightings around the world and a dedicated (if under-funded) ministry within the government. There are pages of information on the Internet about the relatively new science of Zombiology. In particular, check out any work by Dr Kaleed Ahmed.

▶ The so-called "zombic condition" is caused by a complex RNA virus, typically spread by bite or other fluid exchange. There is nothing supernatural about this very real threat to humanity. Most zombiologists (yeah, that's a word) are waiting for that term "the big one" – that is a significant outbreak which overwhelms countries, even the world.

▶ Once infected, a human will typically transform into a zombie within 24 hours after exhibiting a series of flu-like symptoms. Once turned, zombies are slow and unbalanced with a vacant gaze and pallid, almost blue complexion. You cannot cure a zombie.

▶ Zombies hunger for human flesh and are relentless in their single-minded quest to feast on the living. They are no great thinkers but with their jagged finger nails, broken teeth and, above all their numbers, they are a very dangerous opponent.

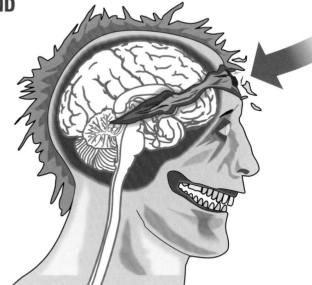

HOW TO KILL A ZOMBIE

Remember, the walking dead are not supernatural beings, they are not the undead. You can kill a zombie by destroying at least 80% of its brain function. Put another way – bash 'em hard in the head with something big and they will be stopped.

ZOMBIE CAPABILITIES

It's vital that you understand the physical capabilities of the walking dead. There are different forms of zombies but, as a rule, they cannot run, use ladders, ride bikes, or jet off for sneaky weekends in the country. Slow, pondering and remorseless – that's them.

ZOMBIE ENERGY

Zombies conserve energy by entering a catatonic state. Little is known about the digestive process of the walking dead. No researcher has really fancied taking the job on.

ZOMBIE SPEED

A whole body zombie will typically amble along at a below average walking pace. They are capable of bursts of greater speed if motivated by the prospect of human meat.

ZOMBIE AGILITY

Zombies do not feel pain so the loss of a foot or whole limb does not prevent movement. Unstable at the best of times, however, zombies with missing body parts will be reduced to moving at a snail's pace, sometimes even reduced to crawling along the ground like a putrid worm.

ZOMBIE BRAINPOWER

The walking dead aren't going to win any pub quizzes but they have the brain capacity to engage arms and legs to drive movement. They are capable of basic shambling but actions such as jumping can cause issues.

ZOMBIE SENSES

Our best research indicates that humans become chronically short-sighted after infection. Zombies therefore have poor eye sight at a distance. Their sense of touch is also diminished. However, they seem to develop a keen sense of smell, particularly for the scent of living human flesh.

THE WALKING DEAD WILL ALWAYS MOVE TOWARDS THE LIVING WITH THE EXPRESS PURPOSE OF TURNING THEM INTO THEIR NEXT MEAT SNACK.

ZOMBIE SPEED TEST

In August 2016, the Ministry of Zombies teamed up with the Royal Jordanian Broadcasting Corporation (RJBC) to make a unique documentary which, working under scientific instruction, sought to examine the different performance capabilities of the main types of zombie – a vital factor when considering transport issues in the aftermath of a zombie apocalypse.

A number of zombie specimens were obtained, categorized, and then assessed in a series of physical tests jokingly referred to by the film crew as the Zombie Olympics. Over a period of several weeks, the study sought to establish performance credentials for the various types of zombie. Crucially, this information could help survivalists answer the age old question – do zombies shamble like in the George A. Romero films or race like sprint runners as in *28 Days Later*.

There is no official test evidence on kiddie ghouls as awkward World Health Organization (WHO) legal restrictions prevent testing but most preppers swear that they are faster than regular zombies and more dextrous.

0–1 MPH
CRAWLERS
(SCRAPPERS, SNAKIES, DRAGGERS)

Typically, crawlers are missing their legs or the entire bottom section of the body. Technically speaking, crawlers could be dragging remaining body parts such as legs dangling on a tendon or stray intestines.

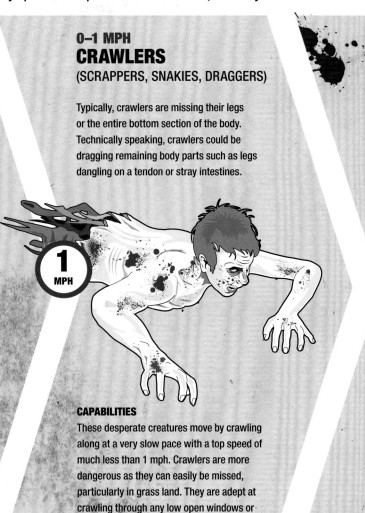

1 MPH

CAPABILITIES
These desperate creatures move by crawling along at a very slow pace with a top speed of much less than 1 mph. Crawlers are more dangerous as they can easily be missed, particularly in grass land. They are adept at crawling through any low open windows or even unprotected ventilation ducts. Do not underestimate these creatures.

2–3 MPH
FRESH OR CLASSIC
(NOOBS, NEWBIES, MUNCHIES)

A classic blue-grey skin colored zombie will be the most common type of ghoul.

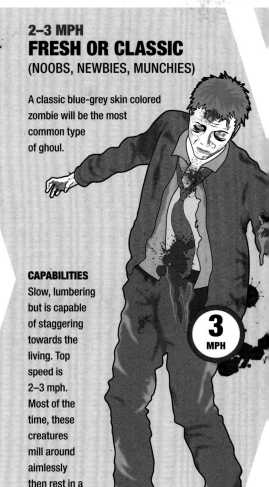

3 MPH

CAPABILITIES
Slow, lumbering but is capable of staggering towards the living. Top speed is 2–3 mph. Most of the time, these creatures mill around aimlessly then rest in a dormant state until alerted by noise or scent.

GETTING AROUND IN ZOMBIELAND
BEWARE OF SEVERED HEADS

Zombie heads can survive for weeks when severed from the infected body and are a surprisingly dangerous form of the walking dead. Severed heads are particularly common in the early weeks of the apocalypse as amateur zombie bashers often believe that decapitation alone will "kill" a zombie.

Severed heads are basically snapping jaws and so can only move through this action. They are therefore capable of rolling slowly towards a target but in most cases they are unable to move more than a foot. Instead, they tend to "sit" and wait for victims.

3–4 MPH
LIMBLESS WONDERS
(DUMMIES, BIRDIES)

Missing both arms and thus carrying less weight. A lack of arms also seems to improve the dead's balance by changing its center of gravity.

CAPABILITIES

Still slow but can reach speeds of 3–4 mph, with one report of 5 mph being achieved. Their main weapon is now just biting. There are countless variations of limbless zombies who are missing major body parts yet are still able to function – these include the legless variety, who move in a similar way to crawlers.

4 MPH

4+ MPH
INFECTED HUMAN
(DEADS, VIROS)

Humans infected with the zombic virus are likely to be panicky and desperate. Some will display bite marks, others no sign at all of infection.

CAPABILITIES

Enhanced human abilities, fuelled by an adrenalin rich surge caused by their recent infection. Psychological studies have shown that, despite their knowledge of infection, infected humans will move into a denial stage in which they may convince themselves that they are somehow immune or uninfected. During this time, they will be capable of any crime to keep their infection a secret, including murder.

4+ MPH

GETTING AROUND IN ZOMBIELAND

THE RIGHT VEHICLE FOR YOU

There are many factors to consider when deciding on your choice of vehicle for the zombie apocalypse. It is advised that you use this volume like a workbook – keep a note pad handy and write down the factors critical to your plans. Read the case studies through and look at the plans before deciding on the right transport mix or vehicle for you. Remember that many preppers will keep a range of vehicles – something light for foraging in the immediate area and a more serious vehicle for bugging out.

ESSENTIAL FEATURES

Inexperienced zombie preppers often skip any detailed analysis and move right on to selecting the vehicle they think will do the job during a zombie outbreak. Indeed, there are Internet forums filled with debates about on-road versus off-road capability, whether new sports utility vehicles can really do the job and if adapting a heavy goods vehicle to create the ultimate fighting platform could really work. There are hundreds of options out there from your old Honda Civic with some barbed wire wrapped around it to a fully equipped gyrocopter.

Whatever vehicle or vehicles you select, here's a checklist of important features. Obviously, if it's just an off-road scrambler you intend to use for foraging then you won't need all this kit, but for any longer-distance travel start here then take out elements if they're not required. You'll come across countless guides and top 10 lists as you develop your skills as a survivalist. Use this information and any others you find as source material and adapt according to your own needs.

▶ On-board Bug-Out Bag
▶ Drinking water for at least 48 hours
▶ Emergency rations for at least 48 hours
▶ Clubbing weapons such as wrenches or baseball bats
▶ Any firearms you can get your hands on
▶ Sleeping bags and blankets
▶ Survival tool box with spare vehicle parts
▶ Emergency first aid kit
▶ Cans of fuel
▶ A selection of maps
▶ Winch and ropes if you have the space
▶ A few spare tins of food for bartering

1. TIME

A very practical consideration. No one knows when the zombies will strike. It is most likely to be in the next 10 years but no one knows for sure. So, you need to be able to commit the time and resources to maintaining your vehicles, including training and all of the other associated costs.

2. BUDGET

A major limiting factor for most. You'll find options easily costing $100,000 in this book but this kind of expense just won't be feasible for everyone. The good news is you don't need to spend big but you do need to spend wisely. For example, it may be cost effective to select one of the conversion kits outlined later and fit it to your current car when the dead rise.

3. THE PLAN

Staying put or Bugging-Out? It's pointless investing in a fully apocalypse-ready recreational vehicle if you intend to fortify your home and then only later venture out into your local area. Consider your options carefully – you can assess your transport needs once you have a strategy.

8. MAINTENANCE

Something which has become more relevant in recent years with the computerisation of many modern cars. Some preppers deliberately pick pre-1980s vehicles because they can be maintained with non-specialist tools. Others tear out the unnecessary tech components on their vehicles hoping to make them easy to maintain and resistant to features of the apocalypse such as electromagnetic pulses (EMPs).

7. FUEL

There's a serious choice to be made here. You'll find a whole section on fuel types in this book but it's a subject on which few zombie preppers agree. Gas, diesel, or alternative – it's a personal choice – each have their advantages and disadvantages. You should consider fuel storage and access to further supplies.

CHOOSING THE VEHICLE OR VEHICLES YOU WANT TO FACE THE END OF THE WORLD IN IS ONE OF THE BIGGEST DECISIONS YOU'LL EVER MAKE AS A ZOMBIE PREPPER.

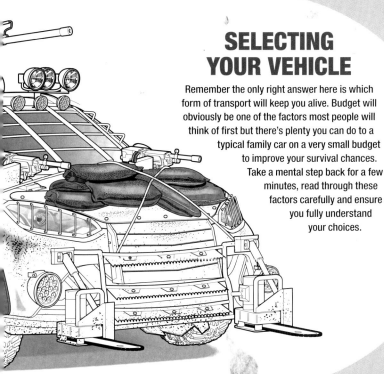

SELECTING YOUR VEHICLE

Remember the only right answer here is which form of transport will keep you alive. Budget will obviously be one of the factors most people will think of first but there's plenty you can do to a typical family car on a very small budget to improve your survival chances. Take a mental step back for a few minutes, read through these factors carefully and ensure you fully understand your choices.

6. LOCATION

Exactly where do you call home? If you live on an isolated farm then you have a good chance of keeping an apocalypse gyrocopter under wraps and secure until it's needed. If you live in the city center, you're likely to need a robust road warrior to battle the inevitable rise of the street gangs. Also, think about where you are going to store your vehicle.

5. BLEND IN

Consider going for a basic model to blend into the apocalyptic background – great for either looting or bugging out over a serious distance. Or, would you prefer to display your post-apoc credentials and weapons with pride, to deter any would-be attackers?

4. SIZE OF GROUP

Are you flying solo or do you have a family to consider? Exactly who will be using your Bug-Out Vehicles? You may need several if you plan to travel as a group or in convoy. Some preppers prefer to invest in a group of vehicles to ensure that they're not left stranded. But others insist Bug-Out Vehicles like converted coaches will be unstoppable in the wasteland, operating like powerful tanks to crush the zombies.

REMEMBER

Keep your working plans confidential. In any conversations with mechanics or garages you can always say you're considering taking up racing.

BASIC TRANSPORT

Here in the United States, there aren't many car showrooms demonstrating the latest Mad Max style road warrior vehicle. As a continent we are poorly prepared in terms of transport requirements. So, let's start at the beginning.

This book is not a zombie survival manual for beginners. We are going to assume that if you have read this far, you're already aware of the importance of keeping fit and active as you prepare for the inevitable zombie apocalypse. So, you should already be familiar with an established fitness regime which includes walking or trekking practice. Regardless of whether you face the apocalypse with a fully pimped apocalyptic tank or an old Nissan Micra with a few pieces of barbed wire nailed on, there will be times when your primary form of transport is by foot. Remember to try to get at least a 6–8 mile training walk in every week as part of your training regime.

▶ This section will look at a number of unpowered transport options including animals and bicycles – two methods often mentioned on zombie prepper forums.

▶ Don't forget that there are other options to support you if you are on foot such as various handcarts – although if you do plan to travel the wasteland with a pimped Tesco shopping cart as your vehicle of choice then this probably isn't the book for you.

▶ Easily available before the dead rise and after Z-Day, you can simply check out any DIY store to get yourself a cart.

▶ Even if it's not your primary form of transport, it is worth grabbing one and keeping it in the trunk of your main vehicle.

OPTION 1
HANDCARTS

Not really a "form of transport" but if you are planning to travel a short distance to, for example, an improved location, survival experts swear by this kind of vehicle. Human-powered, they make surprisingly light work of your supplies should you need to relocate. Not ideal if you are in a hurry but easy enough to just drop should you need to if any zombies shamble too close for comfort. Industrial jumbo hand-wagons can handle loads up to 1,000 pounds – that's a lot of Bug-Out Gear but realistically your range will be limited to a few hundred feet. Easily available before the dead rise and after, you can simply check out any DIY store and help yourself to a cart.

 Handy for moving supplies and looting but, come on, is this really how you imagined the end of the world to be? Is this really the form of transport you wanted to end up with?

OPTION 2
SACK TRUCKS

Similar to handcarts, these can be found in most factories and warehouses. Again, survival experts make good use of these kinds of tools for moving kit around. You won't exactly look like Mad Max dashing between Bug-Out locations with a sack truck stacked with boxes but consider that if you do your back in lifting a heavy load in normal life, for sure it's painful but not a huge issue with access to medical and healthcare resources, but if you do yourself a serious injury in zombie-country then you could end up a very cheap meat snack. A quality handcart or sack truck will enable you to safely move far more Bug-Out supplies than say a back-pack.

 Again, not the best option if you are going for that cool, road warrior vibe but maybe the supplies you forage will keep you alive.

OPTION 3
ADULT SCOOTERS

Seen in every park and playground across the country, scooters also come in robust adult versions. In particular, "Dirt Scooters" are very different beasts from your typical pink-tasselled Anna and Elsa Pink Magic Scooter. These machines are built with serious off-road conditions in mind and for around $500, you get rugged over-sized pneumatic tires, beefy chrome handlebars, and a hardened steel tube frame. Made for stunt riders, these scooters are ideal for short-range foraging trips and are tough enough to see you through an apocalypse. Add a stylish canvas front-bag and scary warning horn to provide your scooter with a more "end of the world" feel.

 A useful option and can cover some good distances but a high center of gravity makes them vulnerable. Plus, you'll look a bit of a fool scooting through the wasteland.

BASIC TRANSPORT
KNOW YOUR LIMITS

The Health and Safety Executive estimates that over 30,000 people are seriously injured in bicycle related accidents every year and a further 14,000 in skateboard or scooter incidents. A startling 391 people were killed in Sack Truck Accidents (STAs) across the country in 2016 alone. If you are opting for any form of transport which relies on you to power it, remember to be fully aware of how to safely operate and maintain your "vehicle." Your own physical fitness will also be an important factor. Overloading your handcart or running out of air as you cycle uphill could easily get you munched in a zombie-ridden wasteland.

SKATEBOARDS ARE UNSTABLE, UNPREDICTABLE, AND PRONE TO GOING OUT OF CONTROL – THOSE NEW TO SKATEBOARDS WILL NOT SURVIVE LONG IN THE WASTELANDS.

OPTION 4
SKATEBOARDS

There are some serious skateboard models out there which can enable you to travel serious distances at a good pace. However, there are two serious survival issues with skateboards. Firstly, whereas a scooter can be mastered in a few days, a skateboard takes substantially longer and it's much easier to have an accident if you don't know what you are doing. Secondly, many skateboards have toughened plastic wheels which make enough noise to draw in any zombie in the vicinity. If you're an expert, you'll be travelling fast enough to dodge them. If not, you could end up with a trail of dead followers, just waiting for you to trip up on the nearest kerb.

Skateboards are hard to master and it's far too easy to have a serious fall. Add to this the fact that most skateboards are noisy enough to attract every zombie in a mile radius.

OPTION 5
ROLLER BLADES

From 1970s-style disco roller skates to modern high-tech in-line skates, there is no shortage of options for when you want to attach small wheels to your feet and speed your way out of trouble. And, with experienced skaters hitting average speeds of up to 15 mph, roller blades might be the solution to outrunning the dead and even bandits. But, it's not for the amateur. Roller skating is one of those things – easy to try – hard to master. It is recommended that you get at least 8 hours practice skating in per week if you plan to use any form of skates as your post-apocalyptic transport. Also, don't forget to practice carrying your full Bug-Out Kit.

Practice makes perfect with any form of roller skates so if you plan to use them to escape the zombies, better get out there now and start to boogie.

OPTION 6
CYCLING

Modern mountain and all-terrain bicycles have quickly become a vehicle of choice for those concerned about blocked roads or fuel supplies. Even if your primary vehicle is motorized, getting your hands on the latest folding survival bike is a sensible back up option. Hard wearing, tough and easy to maintain, these bicycles can cover most ground types and easily outpace the walking dead. Ensure you get the right model so be on the lookout for a light but strong aluminium frame and features such as zombie-repellent horns. There is a near infinite range of cycles out there from standard two wheels to specialist survival bikes.

The right choice of survival bicycle will see you through the zombie apocalypse in style but get plenty of fitness training in before the dead rise.

BASIC TRANSPORT

BIKES AND CYCLING

Cycling will be a very practical way to get around once civilization collapses. Cycles are found everywhere, are easy to maintain and with storage panniers attached there can be room for some foraged booty. Choosing wisely will be important or you could end up battling a group of desperate survivors on a pink Halfords Twinkle. Cycling is well covered on zombie survival forums and most topics focus on mountain or all-terrain bikes which have robust frames and useful gearing. Equally important is personal fitness – a factor often overlooked.

For a reasonable cost, it's possible to kit an entire family out with specially built Bug-Out Survival Bicycles such as the Z-Navigator Folding Bikes (PZ-17) made by the very successful Flying Pigeon Bicycle Company in China. This all-terrain bike and its accompanying children's versions are possibly the best selling survival bicycles of all time. However, you can get some of the same benefits by adapting your own bike, as long as you start with a robust model and consider zombie-gunk proofing the gears and brakes.

▶ INDIAN ARMY HAVILDAR QUADCYCLE

The army of the Republic of India is one of the largest organizations in the world, with well over 1.3 million soldiers and support staff in service at any one time. It has been widely respected around the world for its prowess in emergency planning since a commission was set up in 2010 to look at how the nation should prepare for a major viral outbreak, and it's no surprise that the planning team immediately turned to the power of the bicycle, or more accurately, the quadcycle. The challenge was simple but on an enormous scale. With over a billion people living in a vast country, how could the armed services maintain law and order in the chaotic environment of a zombie outbreak? With nothing suitable available on the open market, they turned to Indian manufacturer Tata Steel to create a unique post-apocalyptic vehicle.

"THE HAVILDAR QUADCYCLE IS CHEAP TO BUILD AND EASY TO MAINTAIN. A THREE MAN RELIEF TEAM CAN TRAVEL SAFELY FOR HUNDREDS OF MILES ACROSS ZOMBIE-INFESTED TERRITORY."
COLONEL "SPOKES" SHARMA

INDIAN ARMY HAVILDAR QUADCYCLE (LIGHT SURVIVAL VEHICLE 713TC)
Indian Armed Forces, Republic of India

LOCATION
Plans held in the Bursar's Office, Rashtriya Indian Military College, Dehradun

PURPOSE
A dependable light transport vehicle, designed for human-powered patrol and reconnaissance duty. Unofficially, it is believed this vehicle is at the heart of the Republic of India's national zombie survival plan.

TECHNICAL SPECIFICATIONS
Gusseted, reinforced steel frame, aluminium alloy floorboard and panels. Steel component front zombie guards, chain-guards and brake arms. 10-speed gearing system. Base model weight 233 pounds, Indian Army Havildar estimated weight 330 pounds. Length 75 inches, width 50 inches, height 72 inches.

ARMAMENTS
Standard configuration with options to add any weapons carried by the riders – two Glock 17 semi-automatic pistols, fittings for an IMI Negev light machine gun, plus an AK-47Z on the back shelf.

RANGE
400 miles with basic maintenance. Service every 500 miles depending on usage.

CREW
2–4 with kit. 3 in survival configuration with one sleeping zone in the rear.

BUDGET
The Indian Army forces have declined to answer this question. A standard base model quadcycle from a quality Italian manufacturer will cost around $7,800. Extras to bring it up to the specification of the Indian Army Havildar Quadcycle could cost as much as $13,000.

USAGE GUIDELINES
Colonel "Spokes" Sharma – "Indian military forces currently have 10 Havildar Quadcycle deployed, with a further 200 being built. All 10 vehicles are with the Sikh Regiment and are under trial. We firmly believe that in a post-apocalyptic scenario, being able to move troops and supplies quickly and without a reliance on either fuel or electronic subsystems, will enable us to maintain law and order and provide relief. I believe it's no exaggeration to say that this vehicle could save the Republic by stemming the tide of the walking dead."

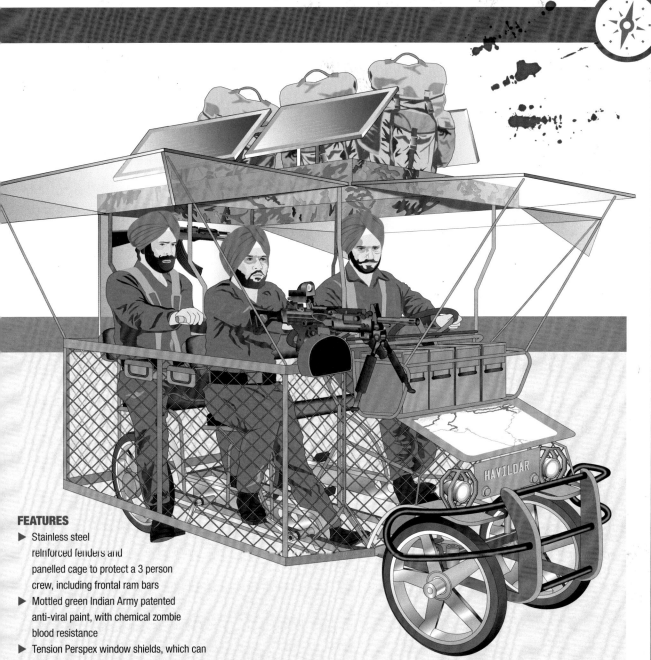

FEATURES

- ▶ Stainless steel reinforced fenders and panelled cage to protect a 3 person crew, including frontal ram bars
- ▶ Mottled green Indian Army patented anti-viral paint, with chemical zombie blood resistance
- ▶ Tension Perspex window shields, which can be lowered to seal the vehicle if required
- ▶ Directional LED head, tail and search lights for emergency rescue missions
- ▶ Integrated 10-gear sealed drive system, based on 2 active peddlers and 1 slave pedal unit
- ▶ Aluminium alloy floorboard and tubular body, offering a robust anti-roll unit
- ▶ Four wheel drum brakes with anti-zombie gunk seals
- ▶ Ultimate Tata-K 'mag' wheels with strengthened Vishna brand tires

- ▶ Forward mounting for light machine gun, with ammunition box feed storage just below
- ▶ Quad solar panels supplying power to a control array on the front control panel. The controller can direct power to lights and a military-grade satellite navigation system
- ▶ Secure roof storage area for soldiers' kit. Standard emergency Bug-Out Supplies include food, water and a purification unit to supply 4 people for up to a week.

TRIALS REPORT

In January 2017, a 3-man crew from 4th Battalion Sikh Regiment took a Havildar Quadcycle on a 400 mile journey, maintaining a constantly moving vehicle over the complete 6 day journey. The crew rode in 4-hour shifts, using a 2-seat survival configuration, with a sleeping space behind. The vehicle averaged a steady 3 mph and was in continuous use. The men ate and slept on board the quadcycle.

BASIC TRANSPORT

BMX RAIDING

Zombie preppers rarely consider a full-sized BMX when making their Bug-Out plans but these robust off-road and trick bikes have much about them to recommend, particularly if used in groups for raiding or foraging purposes. BMXs come in several model types – ideally, you'd be looking for a quality "dirt style" bike which has tires with a deeper tread for better off-road maneuverability. Good jumping ability, robust build quality and a very tight turning circle make BMXs suitable for all sorts of urban activity and models such as the Shimano Apocalypse X even provide a little storage in specially designed mini panniers. BMXs such as the Shimano Apocalypse range cost in excess of $1,300 per bike but a decent model can be picked up for a fraction of the price. It is worth checking online to study the BMX raiding techniques of gangs such as the London-based Krucial Krew, who operated in the mid-1990s pioneering BMX combat techniques such as the "hop out of danger," "death wheelie," and "rotter slap."

BASIC TRANSPORT
APOCALYPSE CYCLING

In March 2017, *Survivalist Monthly* asked its over 8,000 readers which form of bicycle would be their ideal choice for an apocalypse. No reference was made to zombies but the results still confirmed that most preppers opt for a "do it yourself" adapted mountain bike as opposed to a purpose built bike such as the Z-Navigator PZ-17 or any other model type.

3% **ELECTRIC-ASSIST BIKE**
"Economical and quiet, these bikes will gently motor you out of trouble."

5% **PURPOSE-BUILT APOCALYPSE MOUNTAIN BIKE**
"This is the only model I'd go for, something with a good range in case my main vehicle breaks down."

8% **BMX OR SIMILAR**
"I plan to stay in an urban environment so I need something cheap and robust."

13% **FOLDING BIKE**
"It's certainly not stylish but it fits in the back of my Bug-Out Vehicle and provides another transport option if needed."

71% **A STANDARD MOUNTAIN/ ALL-TERRAIN BIKE**
"Pimped with my own added adaptations."

MINISTRY OF ZOMBIES

SURVEY FROM *SURVIVALIST MONTHLY*, MARCH/APRIL 2017 – 2,167 RESPONDENTS

THE CASSIDY APOCALYPSE SHOPPING CART

In late 2015, the Ministry of Zombies sponsored a series of zombie combat workshops for the elderly entitled "Senior Citizen, Senior Survivor." They taught the fundamentals of zombie combat including how to use accessories such as walking sticks and zimmer frames to deal with the walking dead. At the Belfast session, one 81-year-old grandmother shocked the trainers by turning up with a loaded antique blunderbuss gun. Mrs Eileen Cassidy went on not only to demonstrate her black belt in karate but showed designs from her own range of survival wheeled shopping carts known as "Cassidy Carts."

USAGE GUIDELINES

The shopping cart is dual purpose and can be used to either transport supplies such as tea and biscuits or, once a small seat is added, be used to ferry babies and toddlers around. "The first change we made to the basic 'Budget Model' cart was to fix those bloody wheels," reports Mrs Cassidy. "No more wayward steering. These carts stay on course. A nice man from BAE Weapons Systems helped me fit some front rocket launchers and fine-tuned my designs for a street-legal multi-flare gun. This cart will see you through the apocalypse whether you are foraging for supplies at your local supermarket, battling the zombies, or dealing with some bad guys – you'll be prepared."

"WE DO NOT APPROVE OR SANCTION ANY OF MRS CASSIDY'S ADAPTATIONS TO OUR STANDARD CART DESIGN. HER CART IS A MENACE AND DOWNRIGHT DANGEROUS IN THE WRONG HANDS."
MICHELLE LEWIS, CART SOLUTIONS DIRECTOR, CART SOLUTIONS LTD

FEATURES

▶ Titanium steel alloy frame with a secret ingredient added by Mrs Cassidy before assembly (scone crumbs)
▶ Generous Bug-Out Storage Pouch for up to 72 hours of supplies
▶ In-built camelback water pouch plus purification unit
▶ Thermal tea cup holder
▶ Hobnob or Rich Tea pouch
▶ Waterproof scratch card pouch
▶ Available in black or mottled combat camouflage
▶ Four wheel assembly – all can turn 360 degrees for agility
▶ Spiked rear wheels enable users to deploy a "high flick" sending the cart into any approaching zombie
▶ Shotgun pouch

▶ Clubbing weapon holder
▶ Emergency sheet converts the cart into a temporary shelter
▶ Triple stun grenade holder
▶ Emergency smoke deployment unit, trigger is located on the handle

Since 2015, Mrs Cassidy has been just as busy and has recently been working with famous children's buggy empire McLaren to create a pilot "Apocalypse Shopping Cart." These trolleys will come equipped with enough firepower to take on the zombie horde but also a range of educational toys to distract your toddler as you battle through the smoking wasteland. Mrs Cassidy has been working with her daughter-in-law Lauren on this project but things have been slow as Lauren is currently getting an extension to her house. "It'll be nice for the summer," reports Mrs Cassidy, "but I really think she could have planned the building work more carefully."

BASIC TRANSPORT

COPING WITH DISABILITIES

The Ministry of Zombies has worked for many years with disability charities and other organizations to support the very active debate around how those with disabilities can survive a zombie apocalypse. Up to 2010, much of this work was academic and followed UN guidelines in areas such as using a white sheet to call for assistance and waiting for help to arrive. A meeting with Captain Steve "Rusty" Langdon in 2011 changed everything. This 35-year-old US Gulf War veteran was the first to create a purpose built zombie-fighting wheelchair and has continued his work, developing a fully integrated survival scooter. But, before we get into the mechanics, it's worth considering Rusty's three key pointers.

▶ **GET INTO THE RIGHT MIND-SET FROM THE START**
The zombies don't care if you have a disability. You have to rely on yourself and any trusted friends. Get educated. Get trained. Get prepared.

▶ **CONSIDER CAREFULLY YOUR OWN NEEDS**
Think long-term. Stock up on any medication you need. Select the right mode of transport for your situation. I'm unable to use my legs so the Zomb-Chair is ideal.

▶ **ON Z-DAY, EVERYTHING CHANGES**
Sure you'll still have a disability but with your training and a bit of luck, you'll also be a survivor, just like all the other survivors. Use your skills to team up with others – don't be a victim and be prepared to fight to survive.

▶ THE STANNA WASTELAND SURVIVAL SCOOTER

The Stanna Wasteland Survival Scooter is a next-generation personal mobility solution for the zombie apocalypse. It features a powerful battery-powered engine and a host of anti-zombie features, as well as being an impressive wasteland cruiser. Developed by Gulf War veteran and Disability Survival Champion Steve "Rusty" Langdon and Stanna Mobility Solutions, it was built to cope with anything the end of the world can throw at you. "A few years ago, I was part of the team that created the Zomb-Chair. I took a bit of flak as it was considered pretty expensive so teamed up with a commercial manufacturer and together we cooked something up which might just rock your world."

"HAVING A DISABILITY DOESN'T HAVE TO MAKE YOU A TARGET. THERE ARE PLENTY OF ABLE-BODIED PEOPLE OUT THERE WHO ARE POORLY-EDUCATED AND ILL-PREPARED FOR THE ZOMBIES."
STEVE "RUSTY" LANGDON

THE STANNA WASTELAND SURVIVAL SCOOTER
Patent holder: Steve Langdon, Arizona. Licensee Stanna Mobility Solutions

PURPOSE
Short-range post-apocalyptic personal transporter

TECHNICAL SPECIFICATIONS
Overall height 54 inches, width 30 inches, length 63 inches. Maximum gradient 10 degrees, driven by 4 x 75 Ah Supa-Z Sealed Apocalypse batteries. Ground clearance 3 inches. Includes dashboard LCD display, reporting on the 22 zombie-movement detecting sensors set around the vehicle.

ARMAMENTS
None as standard but plenty of upgrade options including rear-shooting nail-gun, M16 fixing point, shotgun pouch and arm-rest bolt gun. Most of the customers to date are happy to manage their own weapons configuration. Anything supplied directly from Stanna must meet the legal requirements for the country it is being imported into.

RANGE
A typical mobility scooter will manage around 10 miles at a steady speed of 4 mph but the Stanna Wasteland Survival Scooter has quadrupled the power of a standard model and in tests has comfortably managed 100 miles, with a cruising speed of 5–6 mph. It has a top speed of 10 mph, more than enough to outrun any zombies. There are plans for a larger gas-engine model from mid-2018 onwards.

CREW
1 plus Bug-Out Bag and support goods. Will run with another person if required but range is reduced.

BUDGET
For a standard base model, built to order, $6,500 plus delivery. A Motability grant may be available in some areas, users may be entitled to a free unit via their NHS Disability Zombie Awareness Scheme.

BASIC TRANSPORT

DISABILITIES

Many disabled zombie preppers go down the 'staying put' route, with a focus on home fortification and laying down stores at the expense of any transportation considerations. Vehicles such as the Wasteland Survival Scooter are changing this, with many preppers unwilling to sit waiting for a rescue which they know may never come. Disabled preppers have choices and there is a growing market in adapted survival vehicles, which is opening up all kinds of options.

> "A WELL-TRAINED PERSON WITH A DISABILITY, WHO HAS PREPARED FOR A MAJOR ZOMBIE OUTBREAK, STANDS AN EXCELLENT CHANCE OF SURVIVING THE CHAOS."
> **STEVE "RUSTY" LANGDON**

USAGE GUIDELINES

"The Stanna Wasteland Survival Scooter is the most powerful personal mobility scooter on the market and the only one specially built to cope with a zombie apocalypse and the unique challenges that emergency will bring for those with disabilities. It's tough, it's fast and it's powerful – it's a useful addition to anyone preparing for the wasteland. However, you have to see it as part of your Bug-Out System. This scooter will handle many of your transport needs but you still need to consider fortifying a home base. Think through your re-charging station and get your on-board weapons mix right. I'm a personal fan of a decent shotgun as at least part of your on-board arsenal."

FEATURES

- ▶ Twin rear view mirrors for all-around rear-visibilty plus rear camera
- ▶ Anti-roll back system prevents scooter from rolling backwards on hills. Rear anti-tip wheels as standard prevent the dead pushing the scooter over during an attack.
- ▶ Freewheel facility allows user to roll-down hills as required
- ▶ Full cross-body seat-belt
- ▶ 22 motion sensors set around the vehicle, calibrated to detect both human and zombie movement.
- ▶ Detachable Sensor pickets – stick sensors in ground set perimeter defense
- ▶ Solar charged battery
- ▶ Armoured 360 degree swivel chair
- ▶ Rear anti-tip wheels for extra stability
- ▶ Automatic electromagnetic braking system
- ▶ Rear-firing bolt gun – like a nail gun – spread can be set and fires at different levels.
- ▶ Jacked suspension offering 8 cm ground-clearance, for off-roading
- ▶ Waterproof up to 1 metre
- ▶ Virtually silent battery powered motors
- ▶ Can be dismantled in a few minutes – manufactured in 5 main pieces
- ▶ Puncture proof tires
- ▶ All-weather protective camouflage scooter cape
- ▶ Survival saddle bags
- ▶ Front Combat Basket, with weapons storage option
- ▶ Distraction flares – a set of triple flares on each side.

BASIC TRANSPORT

POST-APOCALYPTIC INVENTIONS

How to get around after a major zombie outbreak is not a new concern for zombie survivalists. Indeed the earliest documentary evidence is from Lady Nora Brightlings's article "Velopeds and Escaping the Blight," published in *Punch* Magazine in 1883 – in it she considers new-fangled free-wheeling bicycles terrifying in London parks but "..a most ideal route from which to flee the recently risen." However, whilst much progress has been made since this time, the road is paved with some of the most stupid and pointless zombie survival travel contraptions. The most ineffective, useless, and in most cases downright dangerous transport options ever. Some of these products are still available, particularly via disreputable online traders.

◤ ANTI-BLIGHT ARMOR

Sir Richard Splashworth took a standard suit of expensive armor and reinforced all of the joints with toughened leather to create one of the first zombie survival suits. He confidently predicted that a knight wearing his armor could continue to travel the land, rescuing those in need. Noble idea.

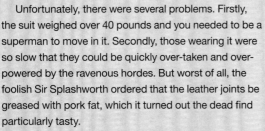

SIR RICHARD SPLASHWORTH HAS SECURED A PLACE FOR HIMSELF IN ZOMBIE FIGHTING HISTORY AS THE CREATOR OF THE WORST OUTFIT IN WHICH TO FACE A ZOMBIE APOCALYPSE.

Unfortunately, there were several problems. Firstly, the suit weighed over 40 pounds and you needed to be a superman to move in it. Secondly, those wearing it were so slow that they could be quickly over-taken and over-powered by the ravenous hordes. But worst of all, the foolish Sir Splashworth ordered that the leather joints be greased with pork fat, which it turned out the dead find particularly tasty.

In summary, it's so heavy you can hardly move, any rain and it rusts, and the zombies just love munching on those pork fat-soaked leather joints. Thanks for nothing Sir Splashworth – avoid this and any modern variations.

◤ GARIBALDI SPRING-SHOES

Advertised in the 1920s as the cheapest way to escape ghouls, inventor Pascal Garibaldi created this apocalypse footwear after seeing a well-known circus act performing with similar mechanisms attached to their feet.

After a few unsuccessful attempts, Garibaldi finally secured a patent on his creation in 1925 and the Garibaldi Spring-shoes were demonstrated at the 1926 World Fair in Philadelphia by famous strongman Fabian McDuff. According to contemporary sources, the giant Scotsman entered a fenced off area with no less than 4 zombies and no weapon. The strongman successfully evaded the ghouls, effortlessly springing over 30 feet in the air and from corner to corner. As an interesting side note, his kilted attire caused something of scandal due to his energetic leaping and is rumored to have caused several female on-lookers to faint.

However, consumer test documents from the time report that the shoes were "uncontrollable," sending the wearer in any direction and at heights of up to 50 feet in the air.

THE PATENT TO THE GARIBALDI SPRING-SHOES IS CURRENTLY OWNED BY THE TRUMP INVESTMENT GROUP.

THE SINCLARE C5Z

Underpowered, with the driver low enough to be within easy grabbing distance of the nearest zombie – even the legless crawling kind – the Sinclare C5z is possibly the worst form of post-apocalyptic transport known to man. To cap all of that, it was sold at the time for a pocket-busting price of almost $4,000 – remember, you could buy a lot of Duran Duran records in 1985 for that price.

Birmingham-based inventor Roger Sutcliffe took a basic Sinclair C5 model, added a 7-foot whip aerial (there is no radio included on the vehicle) and crudely attempted to boost the battery power. The result was a vehicle ill-suited to any post-apocalyptic travel. He also attempted to fool willing buyers by advertising the hopeless vehicle as an official "Sinclare" model, hoping to trade on the early success of Clive Sinclair's C5.

Everything was wrong on the C5z. It was open, slow as a zombie and emitted a low hum which attracted every zombie from miles around. Plus, you look like a right wally driving it. No storage space and a battery guaranteed to leave you stranded. To add insult to injury, models can still be bought online and so the madness of the C5z continues to this day. Beat that world.

THIS DISASTROUS ZOMBIE SURVIVAL VEHICLE IS NOW PERMANENTLY OFF THE ROAD AFTER A SUCCESSFUL LEGAL CASE WAS BROUGHT BY SIR CLIVE SINCLAIR. THANK YOU SIR CLIVE!

SILICON VALLEY SURVIVAL EGG

Designed by some of the smartest beards in Silicon valley, the Survival Egg is $430,000 worth of stick your head in the sand snowflake generation thinking at its best. It's meant to keep the occupant safe in any disaster, from zombies to global warming. A secure high-technology mobile cocoon, with more entertainment options than most homes and even a soothing voice which can be turned on to re-assure the occupant that everything is going to be OK.

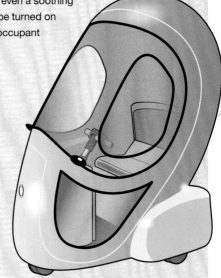

THE SURVIVAL EGG IS THE PRODUCT OF MUDDLED THINKING BY SERIOUSLY INTELLIGENT PEOPLE WITH NO CONCEPT OF THE ZOMBIE THREAT.

Only one problem – it might work on the computer plans but in reality this over priced plastic dome on wheels adapts very poorly in the real world. For that price tag, you could build and equip a powerful Humvee-type Bug-Out Vehicle; instead, here you get a machine which can't help tipping over at the slightest obstruction – even a basic 4 inch curb.

The all-around glass means you're sitting there like a mobile snack for the dead and try downloading the latest driver updates with a hungry zombie slobbering at the window. Whilst the high-tech air conditioning is draining your power, it simultaneously blows unfiltered human-flavored air out, which attracts any zombie within 30 feet of your powered egg-wagon.

Finally, it is equipped with a self-drive AI which seems to veer towards large collections of the walking dead in some bizarre quirk of its on-board machine-learning algorithm.

Little real survival thinking and a major leap backwards in the personal transportation field – an area long explored by zombie survivalists. Forget this fibreglass waste of almost half a million dollars.

BASIC TRANSPORT

HITTING THE ROAD

Modern zombie survival thinking favors a range of vehicles for use during a zombie outbreak but at least one of these should be capable of the longer distances involved in a serious Bugging-Out operation.

Even if you aim to stay put, safely tucked up in your fortified home, things could change, prompting a need for you and your family to move on quickly. Imagine, for example, a wall collapsing and zombies or troublesome bandits intent on looting flooding into your garden. Perhaps there is a polluted water supply making your location untenable. You get the idea. Under these circumstances, we're talking about getting you, your party and supplies possibly hundreds of miles from your home base. This is going to take some serious planning. Most zombie preppers are very secretive about their own Bug-Out plans and you'll find little in the way of route maps or location detail on internet forums.

On our densely populated island, the obvious locations are going to get busy quickly so it's worth crossing off sites such as National Parks. These sites will be crowded with fellow survivors, bandits and, of course, the walking dead. You will need to be more creative, and vehicle selection will be key in guiding any Bug-Out Location decision. Something worth repeating is that you should always have more than one potential location. When considering longer-range Bug-Out Vehicles, focus naturally turns to vans, buses and coaches – larger vehicles with space to store the Bug-Out Supplies necessary for such a journey.

OPTION 1
CARAVANS

If the idea of facing the apocalypse towing a white caravan fills you with dread, your survival instincts are correct… In general, caravans will reduce your carefully prepared Bug-Out Super-Vehicle to the status of an extra-cautious Sunday driver who is being even more cautious than normal as if they are attending some kind of antiques fair. The benefits of bringing your home with you are off-set by the impact on speed and performance. Don't do it, just don't. Go for a campervan/RV instead which offers better stability and road worthiness. A decent caravan could be an option if you have one in place as a hideout in the woods.

The end of the world is no place to try out your sparkling new Coachman Pastiche deluxe caravan regardless of how well its beds fold out or how many toilets it has.

OPTION 2
VANS

With strong frames and decent engines, there are a variety of vans which could be real assets during a zombie apocalypse. Choosing wisely will be the key. It's a very broad market with a few poorly designed and unreliable options out there but get it right and a decent quality van will be an excellent workhouse for carrying supplies. It will blend in well in urban landscapes and can easily be pimped out to become a quality zombie-bashing machine. There are plenty of case studies on the Internet of preppers converting vans into a recreational vehicle or RV configuration, with beds and in-built storage. This often proves cheaper than buying a new RV.

Often over-looked by those new to zombie survival planning, a robust light commercial vehicle provides an excellent base from which to build a suitable Bug-Out Vehicle.

OPTION 3
HGVs

There are hundreds of forum threads discussing the various merits of converting a heavy goods vehicle into a zombie-busting tank and it is a valid point that with the right front protection, these powerful kings of the road could certainly do the business on the walking dead. However, there is less detail on them as long-range bug vehicles. Range is not typically an issue but navigating through our cluttered and blocked roads could present a bigger challenge. HGVs in all their configurations are still a valid option but need to be carefully considered in view of your own location and whether you or your team have the skills to drive one.

HGVs offer some real advantages but these benefits mean that inexperienced preppers tend to overlook the obvious drawbacks in terms of maneuverability.

 MINISTRY OF ZOMBIES

HITTING THE ROAD
HAVE A PLAN

A Bug-Out Location can be something as simple as a secure hideout you can use during an emergency. Some will be very close to your home base. You may even plan to return to your home base once it's safe to do so.

Think of a long-term Bug-Out Location as a resettlement site – somewhere where you can start again, hopefully on more favorable terms with the conditions of the apocalypse. Talk about long-term Bug-Out Locations to any serious zombie survival planner and they're sure to go quiet. It's a personal thing and most prefer to keep their locations secret for obvious reasons. It's a professional courtesy as a fellow prepper to respect their privacy so don't probe.

Once you've decided on a location, remember to do dry runs and even start keeping small stocks of supplies for when things starting turning zombie.

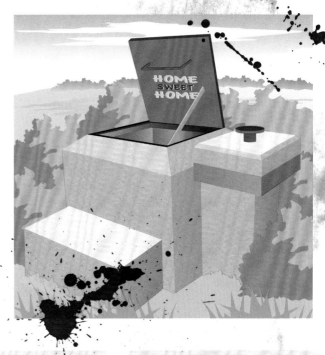

OPTION 4
MILITARY VEHICLES

Forget tanks and many other armored vehicles as most require specialist training, are very rare and have a surprisingly limited range. Hardy models – Army Land Rovers and armored personnel carriers – are often stripped of unnecessary electrical clutter and have easy to maintain engines but they will be highly sought after. Some more well-organized groups will look to use vehicles such as the FV510 Warrior which, with its range of over 400 miles and useful 30 mm L21A1 cannon would prove a powerful protection vehicle for any convoy. In the early days, few groups will have the capacity or organization to take out a vehicle such as a Warrior.

 If you are lucky enough to snag a military vehicle that has firepower then it's a good choice to protect any convoy. Support vehicles are the best targets – Land Rovers or supply vehicles.

OPTION 5
RVs

The zombie survival community takes RVs very seriously and there are now a wide range of apocalypse vehicles available on the market. Even if you decide to purchase a "civilian" model and convert, selecting an RV as your Bug-Out Vehicle is not a budget option and if you settle on a cheaper model, you'll suffer some of the same disadvantages as with a caravan – poor stability, wafer thin fiberglass walls and a lack of defensive features. However, get things right and you'll have made a major step towards surviving the end times. This volume includes a detailed case study of an apocalypse RV – study the features and ensure your vehicle meets this standard.

 A solid, well-built RV is a complete survival vehicle and is a great Bug-Out Vehicle choice. Get the best model you can afford and go for a purpose-built survival vehicle if you can afford it.

OPTION 6
BUS/COACH

Buses and coaches come kitted out for "life on board" with features such as washrooms, seats and even beds – such vehicles feature prominently on most "Best Buy-Out Vehicle" lists. With a reliable bus or coach, you have the prospect of transporting your entire party plus supplies in one main vehicle, perhaps with a few outriders as escorts. That means 1 engine to maintain and 1 fuel gauge to watch, plus the strength of having your forces concentrated in one location. You do need to ensure that your vehicle has some basic defensive features such as a firing platform on top, wheel guards and some frontal protection for ramming.

 Fortified coaches remain a viable option as a larger Bug-Out Vehicle and there is plenty of content out there on survival forums about the conversion process. A good choice.

BASIC TRANSPORT

PREPARING TO MOVE —

Any travel through bandit country is dangerous, but imagine leading a band of survivors including screaming toddlers and Auntie Vi with the bad leg. In addition, you will all be weighed down with any supplies you require for the journey. As with any convoy, you will move at the pace of your slowest member and although the walking dead are not long-distance runners they are capable of overrunning your limited party by sheer numbers. Any members of the party who fall behind will be at the mercy of the following pack of shuffling ghouls. Zombie survival experts cite poor preparation when Bugging-Out as the top cause of avoidable deaths during an apocalypse. No one will be keeping score at the end of the world but this lesson really is one to remember.

HITTING THE ROAD
TOP BUGGING-OUT TIPS

1 As with most areas of survival, planning is key but even preparing a basic movement plan can make for some daunting reading. For example, it will need to include any scouting plans, potential obstacles, your main routes and several alternative routes as they will doubtless be required.

2 You will need to assess your destination and agree any movement plan as well as planning for the unexpected. Tough choices will need to be made on which supplies to take and what to leave behind. The danger, risk, and difficulty of traveling through zombie-infested country increases exponentially with the distance you travel. It is a grim calculation but if you push your party too far or beyond its capabilities, someone will end up getting eaten.

3 In undead America, with roads mostly blocked and even key bridges and tunnels down, your party will probably only average 10–15 miles a day depending on factors such as fitness and ghoul activity. These figures will make long-trek hikes to remote locations such as National Parks or mountain areas an unrealistic objective for most parties.

4 It is good practice to identify at least 3 possible long-term locations before the zombies rise. You can then research these locations in the peace before the crisis and make the best assessment as to their long-term viability.

5 Do as much research as possible. Plot alternative routes and note any sites of potential interest en route. Specific locations will be reviewed in later sections but a good mix of types is important. Above all, do not leave with a general objective to say "get to an island."

6 Your groups should always have a reachable destination and route mapped out. Travel plans will need to change as you encounter the ghouls but your end goal should be clear or people will start to lose faith. Aimless wandering is also a quick way to get members of your party killed. If your current location is overrun and you need to leave in a hurry, head for your nearest Bug-Out Location and re-group before attempting the long-term move.

7 Your choice of long-term locations needs to reflect your party's ability to move so if you know you will be traveling with children or people with movement problems, you need to factor this in. Do not count on any motor vehicles, if you have them then great, but projections are that most carriageways will be blocked. Going by foot or bicycle are good options.

There are many possible scenarios but good planning around emergency bags, escape routes and Bug-Out locations, will give you a fighting chance to reach your long-term destination, even if you need to leave earlier than expected.

► LONG-TERM BUG-OUT LOCATIONS

Emigration
Leaving the country?

Thinking of grabbing a boat and getting abroad? Experts predict that if one major country falls to the zombies, the others will follow closely on in a ghoulish domino effect. If you really desire a move, think through the logistics of even a relatively simple route across the sea. Also, will the desperate survivors in these locations be glad to see you?

Other Towns and Cities
Finding abandoned urban locations

Perhaps other parts of the country won't be hit as hard. For sure, our most populous urban locations will be virtual no-go zones but could smaller locations be more practical? Also, what about making use of our many fortified medieval sites? If you can find, for example, a smaller urban area that was evacuated before the real chaos, you might be lucky and be able to settle in a relatively untouched site with any supplies that were left behind.

Retail Parks and Outlets
Classic zombie survival locations

Most towns and cities now have retail parks on the outskirts so you'd be looking at a much shorter Bug-Out journey. Ample supplies, good defensive potential, and a choice of high street names – what's not to love? Well, if you think that way so will other groups of survivors and bandits. Expect organized gangs to hit these locations and become very protective over other survivors moving in on their turf.

Military Base
Safe and secure?

Reinforced steel outer perimeters and the mouth-watering prospect of military vehicles and weapons make these sites an attractive choice. But remember, these locations are most likely to be a venue for many "last stands" as the brave remnants of the army and desperate survivors battle to the end. Expect these locations to be infested with zombies and the supplies long-since exhausted. Worth a scout but don't expect to settle.

Going Underground
Living like a Morlock

You may be lucky enough to have or know about a secure and prepared luxury bunker. The rumor is that the government has them all over the place. More likely, you'll be facing life in a dark and damp basement-type affair. Bunkers and caves are typically hard to find, plus you'll still need to keep your transportation handy for regular foraging trips. If the kids start developing large saucer eyes, it's time to move on.

"The Country"
Rain boots and the occasional zombie

Most often cited as a Bug-Out location but in reality you are rarely far from an urban center in most of the US. There are areas such as our National Parks but factor in that you'll be sharing the district with thousands of refugees from other areas.

Islands
Protected by the sea or marooned?

Luckily, the US has ocean coastlines, which could provide a refuge from the zombie chaos. The bad news is that the coasts can be difficult to reach.

NOTE: LONG-TERM SETTLEMENT LOCATIONS ARE COVERED IN MORE DETAIL IN THE HAYNES *ZOMBIE SURVIVAL MANUAL*, 2013

BASIC TRANSPORT

LONG-DISTANCE TRAVEL

Regardless of how discreetly you move, the journey of any party of live humans will attract the attention of hungry ghouls and before too long ongoing defenses will be required. It is important to remember, however, that you are not on a crusade against the dead. Your operating guideline is to travel as quietly as possible avoiding hordes where you can and minimizing any encounters. You may need to lengthen your journey to go around urban areas or zombie crowds, for example.

You may also encounter bands of remaining humans who will become increasingly desperate as their struggle to survive gets harder and harder. Again,

avoid encounters if you can by staying clear of the most obvious foraging locations such as shopping complexes or town centers.

If you should directly encounter any other bands of humans, exercise extreme caution. Be friendly where possible and help those in need but be firm. Desperate times will create desperate people. Be sceptical of outsiders; your party will depend on your judgement. If there is any element of confrontation back down if you can and retreat with your supplies and party intact. You should be prepared to fight if rivals attack.

▶ HOW TO STAY ALIVE IN THE WASTELAND

The following guidelines should become second nature as your party transits through bandit country and are the basics of taking a group through zombie-infested areas. Know your group well before you leave and allocate roles to match people's skills. Ensure everyone has a job and knows what is expected of them. There won't be any time for debate once you're out in zombieland.

"ONCE CIVILIZATION HAS COLLAPSED, LONG-DISTANCE TRAVEL WON'T BE FOR THE POORLY PREPARED. PREPARE CAREFULLY. PLAN IN DETAIL. BE READY TO FIGHT AT ALL TIMES."
DAWN JAMES, MOODY'S SURVIVOR GROUP

STEP 1
ALWAYS CHECK VEHICLES

Ensure that you regularly check your main vehicles and be prepared to evacuate one if it goes out of action for any reason. This means ensuring that vital supplies are spread across vehicles and that you have the capacity to lose any one vehicle. Vehicle breakdowns are the most likely source of trouble so ensure that you have a generally understood operating guideline – such as "if it can be repaired in a few hours, we'll do it, if not; we abandon it and move on."

STEP 2
AN EFFECTIVE DEFENSE

All of your party should have some form of defense, like an effective melee weapon, for example, and have the skills to use it. There may be exceptions to this such as very small children or the sick but you must maximize your anti-ghoul arsenal and discourage roving bands of humans from taking advantage. Remember to distribute your best warriors in the convoy system outlined.

HITTING THE ROAD
SCOUTING METHODS

A good technique when heading out on any long-term travel is to use a forward scout to try out potential routes and highlight risks and obstacles before the main party arrives.

▶ Traveling up to a day in front, this pathfinder will check routes and propose changes to avoid blockages. A useful technique is where the guide leaves prominent marks in spray paint along the route to guide the following party. Off-road motorbikes are ideal where longer distances are involved but the noise can be an issue. Bicycles are quieter but slower and have a shorter-range.

▶ Your scout should be fit and a strong fighter. They should be lightly provisioned and armed but their main objective is stealth and research, not engagement. This role demands as much patience as it does strength so discount any gung-ho Rambo types.

▶ With a realistic target location, a good scout may be able to review an entire route to your new location and even transport small quantities of supplies. Other activities may include doing a quick sweep of your target location or preparing a strong point to provide a safe base in your new area. If your party is large enough, then using a scout is strongly recommended.

STEP 3
SPEED IS AN ADVANTAGE

Do not be tempted to over-load your vehicles or party with supplies. In most scenarios, speed will be your principle advantage over the shuffling undead so do not negate this advantage. If necessary, transport supplies on separate runs or, if this is not possible, simply be ruthless with the amount. Over-burdening key members of your team who need to serve on defensive duties could be fatal to your party.

STEP 4
CONTACT STRATEGY

You and your party must develop and agree on a contact strategy for when you encounter the walking dead. For example, the military make good use of pre-agreed hand signals to communicate information from the soldier on point. It is vital that the whole party understands when to stay silent and even when to scatter. A simple set of agreed guidelines in areas such as dealing with an unexpected encounter will greatly increase your chances of survival.

BE AWARE THAT APPEARANCES CAN BE DECEPTIVE
It is possible that you and your party will enter an apparently empty area only to be confronted by ghouls swarming from every building. Do not assume this is some kind of ambush or that the zombies have developed some way to coordinate an attack, it is far more likely that no matter how quiet your party is, their noise or the scent of live humans has just taken time to reach the dormant ghouls. A good way to avoid this is to use a forward scout to make a significant noise and check out a route, as long as he or she can safely exit if numerous ghouls emerge.

TRAVELING WITH ANIMALS

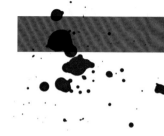

Humans have been using animals for riding and carrying loads for thousands of years so it's worth considering how the animal kingdom can support your post-apocalyptic travel plans.

Before getting carried away with visions of riding into the sunset after raiding a rival survivor camp, slashing zombies with a gleaming sabre as you go, remember that although animals don't need fuel they do need food, water, care, and attention. Also, when we talk about animals we are looking at 2 broad areas: beasts of burden such as donkeys – used to carrying supplies – and animals you can ride, such as horses and camels.

> **"ANIMAL HUSBANDRY WILL BECOME A SKILL THAT IS HIGHLY VALUED IN THE POST-APOCALYPTIC WORLD."**
> JULIAN HENDRY, *SKILLS FOR THE END OF THE WORLD*

If you are looking at using any animal in your Bug-Out plans it's important that you have a thorough understanding of that animal's needs and capabilities, most importantly, how they react to the ever-present zombies. You will need to be experienced in the husbandry, training and care of your animals and have the necessary supplies to keep your beasts fit and healthy. One advantage that animals have is that, to date, no animal has developed the zombic condition. They can contract the virus but for reasons not yet understood, animals do not transform into zombies. The only exception is larger primates but, unless you're planning to monkey-ride your way out of the zombie wasteland, you shouldn't need to worry about luring away any zombie chimps with rotting bananas.

OPTION 1
HORSES

When considering animal transportation, horses are often the first option most survivalists consider. After all, there are almost 800,000 horses in the UK alone and training is widely available, with many stables running short intensive training sessions to help you get started. But how realistic is the horse as a post-apocalyptic form of transport? First point to note is that horses and zombies do not mix well. The rotting stench and groan of the walking dead makes them nervous and flighty. A further development is that there have been reports of zombies eating horses, although this may be to do with the presence of human scent on the animals.

 Their adverse reaction to the walking dead makes them a poor choice for a zombie apocalypse. If you are considering horses, remember to get as much training as possible.

OPTION 2
PACK DONKEY

Fitted with saddlebags, working donkeys are useful pack animals and can be kept as pets providing you have the right set up. The good news is that there are thought to be over 60 million donkeys in the world. Despite being practical working animals, these robust creatures react badly to the walking dead. The lumbering motion and stench of zombies makes donkeys nervous. However, this has not stopped the Chinese Red Army investing heavily in the training of donkeys and mules as transport options, so much so that China now has more donkeys than other country.

 A good option away from the walking dead. Availability is also a key factor however.

OPTION 3
LLAMA

No quips about pan-pipes here as these South American natives are pretty useful beasts of burden. Adult male Llamas can carry around 100 lbs of supplies. They also like carrots, a lot. Reports from Brazil indicate that Llamas are indifferent to the walking dead. These cool creatures aren't bothered by much and sources suggest that their strong odor masks human scent providing another layer of defense. A useful choice and a definite upgrade on the donkey in terms of reactions to the walking dead. These creatures are also adept at navigating most landscapes and can get by with very little in terms of food and water.

 Seriously, Llamas really are through the looking-glass. Unless you are a professional with access to a herd, it's hard to see where you are going to source these robust animals.

 **MINISTRY OF ZOMBIES**

TRAVELING WITH ANIMALS
ZOMBIE RIDING – SPORT OF KINGS?

Popular in California after an outbreak in the 1880s, the infamous Raphael clan specialized in de-nailing and de-toothing zombies, then riling them up in the ring where members of the excited audience could ride the creatures rodeo style.

The powerless zombies could smell the human flesh close to them and this drove them into something of a feeding frenzy but the tragic creatures were unable to feast on it, resulting in a bucking maneuver, producing a realistic "buckaroo" experience. Even if the zombies did manage to close in on a stray arm or leg, the rider would just feel a dry rasping as the zombie lacked any teeth to make the kill. This distasteful sport was banned in 1920s after a high-profile accident involving a budding movie actress, the Bishop of San Francisco, and several de-toothed zombies –although several distasteful homemade video clips appear on YouTube from time to time before being quickly taken down.

WARNING!
THE MINISTRY OF ZOMBIES ADVISE NEVER TO RIDE A ZOMBIE

OPTION 4
DOG SLEDS

Everyone loves dogs but a team of 6–8 Huskies? Aren't they going to eat more food than you can carry on your sled? Unless you live in the Arctic circle, dogs are costly and complex in terms of survival resources. There is specialist zombie training for dogs (see Mrs Woodford's School) and a well-trained dog can be a real asset but don't expect your household pooch to become a zombie-sniffing, ghoul biting super-dog overnight. The process takes months of training. Interestingly, experts say that any dog can pull a sled or cart with the right training and conditioning but in reality many favor larger breeds such as German Shepherds or Dobermans.

 Canines are immune to the zombic condition but keeping a team of dogs in the aftermath will be beyond most survivors. Keep them as guard dogs and companions.

OPTION 5
REINDEER SLEIGH

Here at the Ministry of Zombies, we admit we don't know much about reindeer – only that Santa uses them to pull his sleigh – so we had to call on Scandinavian survival expert Lars Amundsen. Reindeer are certainly an option in some parts of the world but you're unlikely to come across a herd if you live in the city. Amundsen claims they can carry up to 80 lbs of supplies and are useful mountain walkers. The Norwegian Army has used reindeers for transport for many years and has hinted unofficially that the creatures respond well to zombies. Not a realistic option for most in the US but may be an option for our Canadian survivalist cousins.

 Not as crazy as it sounds and everyone loves Christmas. Various military forces around the world who operate in colder climates have teams specializing in reindeer husbandry.

OPTION 6
ELEPHANTS

You might find one in a zoo but, depending on where you are in the world, it may be hard to get hold of one in an emergency situation. Also, can you imagine feeding or even hiding a fully-grown elephant? Unless you are a trained elephant expert, keep away from these majestic creatures. War elephants have been used for thousands of years and in the conquest of the Nanda Empire in 321 BC, both sides are said to have used zombie trained elephants to battle a walking dead outbreak. It's worth remembering that elephants are not counted as domesticated animals – they are in fact wild animals and this nature can make these powerful beasts unpredictable.

 There is a lot of mileage over the longer-term to recreate some zombie-busting creatures of the ancient world. Might be a better long-term project.

TRAVELING WITH ANIMALS

MAN'S BEST FRIEND ——

Since the work of Mrs Victoria Woodford back in the 1970s, preppers have been aware of the use of trained dogs in survival plans. Certain breeds can be trained to sniff out the dead, attack when required and importantly are immune to developing the zombic condition, although they can be carriers of the virus. In terms of transportation, dogs are domesticated enough to travel with us, and some survivalists in northern regions have experimented with dog-sled teams, which are ideal for bugging out over long distances in icy or snowy conditions. However, in terms of carrying gear or supplies, most canines are limited to lighter items placed in specially designed panniers. The ASPCA has a small range of doggie bug out bags specially designed to carry everything a working dog will need over a 48 hour period. There is even space to add in extra water supplies and provisions to support human members of the group.

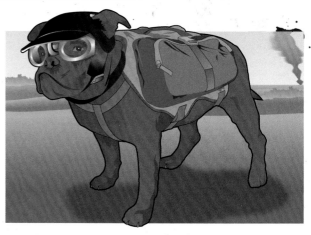

"LOOK AFTER YOUR HOUND AND THEY WILL BE BY YOUR SIDE WHATEVER CHALLENGES THE END TIMES BRING."
MRS VICTORIA WOODFORD,
RSPCA PUBLIC LECTURE SERIES, MAY 1978

TRAVELING WITH ANIMALS
THE POST-APOCALYPTIC ANIMAL ENVIRONMENT

In March 2017, the Ministry of Zombies teamed up with the ASPCA to produce a draft report on how our wildlife would fare during a zombie apocalypse. For the zombie prepper, it's important to know what kind of wildlife profile you'll be facing, and also to start assessing the chances of domesticating any creatures you find roaming the wasteland. Here are the report's predictions on some of the winners and losers.

1 WILD DOGS WILL RULE

Wild dog packs will become a feature of the wasteland. With over 90 million dogs in the US, the end of man could be the start of a new canine age. Expect wild packs of larger dogs as the smaller and domesticated ones won't last long.

2 EMPIRE OF THE RATS

Expert opinion is divided on just how many rats there are in the US, but the end of man will see a boom period for black and brown rats of every size. Numbers will expand exponentially for the first year, with the creatures growing in size and ferocity. They will head out of urban areas and die back as food runs out and they exhaust supplies.

3 CATS ON THE MENU

There are almost 85 million cats in the US but experts predict that this won't save domesticated tabbies from becoming food. Recent tests have shown that zombies will consume cat meat if desperate, as will humans, dogs and just about everything else.

4 AN INSECT SUMMER

Imagine it, the first scorching summer with millions of dead milling around – that's paradise for flies, maggots, and any number of insect pests. Expect swarms to cover parts of the country but these will die out in any colder weather.

5 WILDLIFE RETURNS

One aspect of the fall of man which excited the ASPCA is that the collapse of civilization will likely see the return of some of our endangered species – they highlight otters and barn owls as two creatures which are likely to prosper. We pointed out that everyone getting turned into zombies isn't, however, the best nature conservation scheme on offer. The report was never published.

SINAI ZOMBIE SURVIVAL CAMELS

The noble camel is truly a "gift from God" when it comes to Bug-Out animals. Tall, strong, powerful, loyal, and hardy, these animals have done good service around the world for thousands of years. In addition, camels have always been tolerant of zombies. Unlike horses, they do not find the smell of rotting flesh, the low groan or even the slashing claws of the walking dead alarming and have been used for many years in the Sinai peninsula of Egypt to battle zombies. So much so in fact that region began breeding "zombie-resistant" camels as early as the 1900s and now such animals are available for the first time world-wide.

Genuine Sinai Zombie Survival Camels are available from the Jebaliya tribe in Egypt for as little as $1,300 plus delivery. You should be aware that you will need to meet all legal obligations for the transport and keeping of your camel and that camels generally prefer to be in groups so you may need to consider purchasing more than one. But, for now, enjoy the amazing features of this incredible animal.

These camels are fiercely loyal, particularly the females, and are dependable traveling companions, capable of travelling around 100 miles per day at an arrange speed of 3–4 mph. Although not racing camels, Jebaliya camels can reach up to 12 mph when sprinting.

"TAKE CARE OF YOUR CAMEL AND SHE WILL TAKE CARE OF YOU MY FRIEND. BE ZOMBIES OR DESERT BANDITS, SHE WILL NEVER LET YOU DOWN."
SHEIK MUSSA, JEBALIYA TRIBE, SINAI, EGYPT

FEATURES

▶ Specialized Jebaliya Zombie Saddle – enables the rider to sit high and includes various pouches for Bug-Out Supplies.

▶ The battle saddle comes with a harness for a modern version of the antique Arabic musket specially designed to fire metal anti-zombie balls. Also includes power bag and extra balls. Such a weapon is highly prized in the Sinai and is both hardy and can fire virtually anything, even pebbles.

▶ A Jebaliya camel will hiss and bash its head into zombies on command. It is more than capable of knocking ghouls to the ground and is fitted with a neat leather battle cap.

▶ These camels have been bred to give off a strong pungent odor, which seems to deter the undead.

▶ Each Jebaliya camel can be upgraded with a Bedouin Bug-Out Bag – which is a high-quality low-technology survival kit, designed to pack up and fit neatly into the saddle. It includes a camping rug, goat skin water bottle, and food bag of dried fruits. It is said to be able to keep one survivor alive for several weeks.

▶ Camels are fitted with hardened shoes to cover their pads and to adapt them for urban travel. Once off tarmac, these shoes can be easily removed.

▶ Jebaliya camels do require slightly more water than other breeds but this is still substantially less than other pack or riding animals. A fully grown female can operate for up to 4 weeks without water.

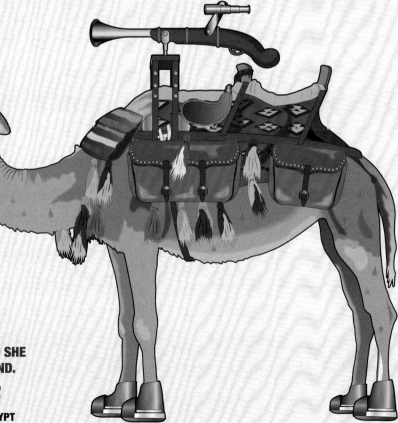

TRAVELING BY WATER

You may be within reach of the coast, river, or canals or waterways. Anything more than a puddle can be a real challenge for the average zombie.

Easy access to a river or waterway could greatly increase your ability to forage and explore further afield. For example, you could use river transport to reach some key supply locations such as large retail stores or warehouses rather than risking a more dangerous road route.

There are countless books and courses which can teach you river craft or how to handle your new small boat but few will prepare you for the unique challenges of the zombies. You must be prepared for the numerous floating corpses which are expected in the aftermath of the ghoul rising and the grim possibility of blocked rivers. Forget any ideas of a pleasant river cruise, there will be the constant threat of ghouls clawing at your paddle or dropping from low bridges. You will need to be vigilant and silent as you move through the water.

WATER ACCESS REQUIRED

Few homes have direct and secure access to a waterway so chances are you will need to lift and carry your boat to the water's edge. This doesn't sound too traumatic but in reality this could be a very dangerous exercise. If you are lucky enough to live somewhere that backs onto a river then don't forget that you will still need to 'secure' your access with strong anti-ghoul fencing.

IS TRAVELING ON WATER SAFE?

It really depends. A waterway clogged with dismembered crawlers, floating limbless wonders, and the occasional bloater on the bank is a far from safe place but water is certainly no friend to the clumsy dead. With sensible precautions, most water forms of transport will be preferable to facing the hungry hordes on dry land. As a general rule, the deeper the water, the safer you'll be.

OPTION 1
SMALL DINGY

In terms of reliable and practical river transport, you will struggle to beat a wooden or fiberglass 2–3 man dingy, which can be bought for around $300 and will provide you with an easy to control craft in which 2 team members could head out in to forage and still have room to bring back valuable suppliers.

Robust and hardy, these crafts are typically light weight and could be easily carried to the water's edge when required. If you decide to use a motorized version, you will need to carefully consider the noise implications against the advantages in terms of distance traveled. Choose a boat with high sides if possible to resist grabbing water zombies.

You need to be physically fit to operate any boat using oars over longer distances so ensure that you get out on the river for training. Some survivalists prefer short kayak paddles to oars as they are more difficult for zombies to grab hold off as you move through the water.

OPTION 2
INLAND MOTOR CRUISER

As an example, there are hundreds of pleasure craft available on locations such as the Norfolk Broads where there are hundreds of miles of navigable waterways and some excellent remote rural locations to moor. The older boats often hired out for holidays are like flat-bottomed floating caravans and are designed to take up to 12 people in relative comfort. With dependable diesel engines and a robust fiberglass build, these crafts could easily provide a floating bastion for you and your team.

Better still, if you can purchase and secure a boat before the zombies arrive, you can stockpile fuel and supplies ready for the crisis. You will then be able to head out to a secure bug out location, moor up and see the crisis through in comfort whilst doing a spot of fishing.

It should be noted that most of the boats on inland waterways are not designed for the open water of the sea but can if stocked up to provide an excellent alternative to a fixed land location.

TRAVELING BY WATER
GET THE RIGHT TRAINING

Before getting carried away, it is important to understand that all types of crafts, bar the very smallest dingy, will need some degree of specialist training, if not to steer then at least to maintain. Consider the treacherous currents around our coast and the problems you may experience navigating, and you will realise that boats are not something you can just jump into.

Whichever craft you select, it is important that you get some experience on the river before the dead rise. Thousands of people enjoy canoeing around the country and it is an ideal way to learn the rivers and waterways in your location. It may be that these routes offer you a more secure trip to a long-term location, for example, in which case, you will need to seriously think about accommodating the whole party and supplies. The options below present some different solutions, including the possibility of securing a much larger vessel that could double as a floating base as well as a form of transport. Don't discount commercial boats as they are often over-looked in favour of more expensive and well-equipped private cruisers.

SEAFARING AND SAILING SKILLS NEED TO BE LEARNED, THEY CANNOT JUST BE PICKED UP IN A FEW HOURS.

OPTION 3
YACHT

Yachts or any sea-going vessels require a substantially bigger investment in terms of money and resources than say fiberglass canoes or smaller craft. The market for private vessels is a very broad one with prices ranging from $5,000 for a used single diesel engine boat, which will still have a kind of floating caravan feel, to the multi-million pound super yachts of the rich and famous, which often include their own pools and be over 525 feet in length.

The good news is that there is a well-established used boat market with prices to suit most budgets. For example, the $5,000 mentioned above could easily secure you a reasonable 30-foot long vessel with a single cabin and which is capable of up to 6 knots. With 13-gallon fresh water tanks and sails to use, it's possible to effectively manage fuel consumption and therefore such a vehicle would be quite capable of long-distance travel – you could easily head out to sea and spend a few relaxing months, waiting for the chaos to die down.

OPTION 4
COMMERCIAL VESSELS

As you move up the vessel price range, new options open up to the zombie survivalist. Even if you mark the luxury yacht market as unrealistic, there is a whole range of medium-priced vessels, which although still require a serious financial investment, will provide you with one of the most secure mobile living spaces. One example is a converted commercial whaler which is on the market for around $250,000 – a substantial commitment for most people.

This particular vessel is over 80 feet long and offers 6 cabins with additional living and storage space. It is a sea-going vessel and a rough calculation on fuel capacity indicates that it could do over 15,000 miles on 1 full tank of fuel. It is possible, particularly if you are part of a larger survival team, that you could pool your resources as this vessel would easily accommodate 15 to 20 people. This opens up the possible strategy of heading to sea for the first few months of the zombie apocalypse and then carefully exploring the coast in the months that follow.

TRAVELING BY WATER

ZOMBIES AND WATER

The dead avoid deep water where possible and they certainly can't swim. This does not necessarily make any lake or river a ghoul-free zone though as they can float in the water and are more than capable of clambering up onto most boats. However, it does mean that if you have access to either the sea or one of our major river or canal systems, then Bugging-Out by water should be investigated.

One aspect that survivors often don't consider is that immersion in water does change the appearance of the walking dead. Bodies typically display a greater degree of ruination and rotting. Green fungus can cover the entire corpse and gases bloat zombies up into significantly larger creatures. Over a period of time, the dead can take on a putrid sea-monster appearance which can shock survivors.

It's almost impossible to prepare survivors for this marine form of ghoul shock. Just remember some basic combat moves and try to disregard their putrid appearance.

For example, an overhead bash is a powerful move almost certain to take out a zombie attacker providing you use a strong, reinforced paddle. The Stab 'n' Poke is an alternative and involves using a paddle or oar to simply jab or push the dead away from the boat.

With each maneuver the objective is to get the ghoul away from the boat and make your escape. Don't become another victim of marine ghoul shock.

▶ A GUIDE TO ZOMBIES IN WATER

TYPE 1
WADERS AND FLOUNDERERS

Experienced zombie fighters often say that shallow water is more dangerous as the dead mill around in water a few feet deep, ready to pounce on any passing human or boat. The water is deep enough to slow the living down and give the clumsy dead a fighting chance of a quick meat snack.

TYPE 2
THE FLOATING DEAD

Most zombie bodies float – meaning they'll drift as quickly as the current takes them, often becoming blocked at narrow points or shallows. Even if you make it to an island, you'll never be truly safe as one of the floating dead could wash ashore at any time. Many corpses can also clamber aboard any boat or raft which sits low enough in the water.

TRAVELING BY WATER
ZOMBIES AND WATER

The Ministry of Zombies Transport Committee published an educational leaflet in early 2017 particularly targeted at educating survivors on the dangers and limitations of zombies and water. Here are some of the key questions:

CAN ZOMBIES SWIM?

We can confirm that zombies cannot swim. They lack the dexterity and the mental capacity to carry out even the most basic swimming stroke. They can wade through shallow water but once it reaches above their waist they are in danger of tipping and floating off. The frequent eye witness accounts of swimming zombies are often floating torsos that have re-animated and now have flaying arms which can suggest the impression of a creature swimming.

ARE ZOMBIES SCARED OF WATER?

Zombies have no emotions as we understand them and are therefore not scared of anything. What is being referred to here is a curious reaction that some of the walking dead have exhibited when confronted with a body of water as an obstacle, particularly if they can see a living human on the other side. Their overriding desire is to feast on the flesh of the living but their limited brain capacity is sometimes confused by the water in front of them.

DO ZOMBIES SINK?

It is true that saturated zombies in heavily waterlogged clothes will generally sink to the bottom. But, typically, currents prevent them from shambling along as normal. However, it should be noted that zombies do not require respiration to exist and therefore it is possible for these creatures to "stay alive" whilst trapped underwater.

TYPE 3
BOTTOM FEEDERS

Some of the dead sink for a reason – they may be wearing heavy body armor or a massive rucksack, for example – and others just become drenched. We may not yet understand the science but the river or ocean bed is not a zombie-free zone and many swimmers will be caught unawares by these carnivorous bottom-feeders.

TYPE 4
BLOATERS

Bloaters are zombies which have, through an internal accumulation of acid and gas, become over-sized, often with vast protruding stomachs. More common in humid climates, these creatures can sometimes be found close to rivers and canals – particularly if the weather is warm. Bloaters are slower moving than a typical zombie.

TRAVELING BY WATER

BUGGING-OUT BY CANOE

For a light and fast option, a well-designed, strong plastic touring or expedition canoe will cost between $500 and $700 and is a craft purposely designed for longer-distance travel. Modern canoes and kayaks can come with all sorts of accessories such as special fixed storage containers etc. What is common to all of these types of small boats is their shallow draft in the water, which will enable you to move on most waterways even if they are only a few feet deep. They can, however, be vulnerable to tipping so you should buy a newer outrigger anti-zombie model such as the Zomboe range. It is possible to modify a standard kayak by fitting an outrigger array but it's a complex job and will involve some specialist tools and skills.

CANOES AND KAYAKS

▶ Combat against human opponents is nigh on impossible from a canoe – particularly if they are armed. If your opponent is stronger or in greater numbers, attempt to escape by water. If you have to fight, make a landing, unseen if possible, then get stuck in. Be extra careful around bridges etc where either bandits or zombies could drop and even overturn your vessel.

▶ Canoes and other boats as Bug-Out Vehicles can be used for the journey but can't possibly be permanent locations. Sooner or later you will need a land base for supplies and repairs. Outrigger canoes are stable and perfect for these kinds of journeys but traveling beyond 100 miles, depending on conditions and levels of fitness, is unlikely.

▶ ZOMBOE 250 SERIES

The Zomboe 250 series is the world's first purpose-built zombie apocalypse outrigger canoe and is built by the Hawaii Watercraft Association in Honolulu. A high-performance, ultra-narrow underwater shaped canoe, a zombie-canoe or Zomboe comes in 1 and 2 person variants, both capable of taking survivors long distances across closed and open waters. Importantly, the outrigger adds the much needed stability that has blighted canoe and kayak forms of transport in zombie testing, where the ghoul simply unbalances the boat.

"AS A PROUD ISLAND PEOPLE WE ARE WELL PLACED TO SURVIVE A MAJOR ZOMBIE OUTBREAK. AND, THE ZOMBOE RANGE GIVES US THE KAYAKS AND CANOES TO DO IT IN."
DUKE AKAKA, PRESIDENT OF HAWAIAN WALKING DEAD DEFENSE GROUP

ZOMBOE 250 SERIES
Hawaii Watercraft Association, Honolulu

PURPOSE
If you plan to use canals, rivers or coastal waters to escape the zombies, this is the ideal cruiser. Stable in the water and fully equipped with emergency supplies, a Zomboe 250 will get you to your Bug-Out Location and can easily be converted into a light raider or patrol boat.

TECHNICAL SPECIFICATIONS
100% carbon layup, titanium shaft, high density foam ocre, one piece monocoque construction plus hybrid anti-zombie marine paint. Length 21", beam 16". Hull weight 19lbs.

ARMAMENTS
Waterproof storage point for handgun. Metal reinforced paddle plus spare.

RANGE
Zombie apocalypse canoeing is very challenging, requiring excellent levels of fitness. In ideal conditions, an experienced rower can travel 2–4 miles per hour.

CREW
1–2 in basic models. Also available in 8-berth models.

BUDGET
Basic model for 1 person $4,000, with zombie apocalypse survival pack. 2-berth variants from $5,000. Larger bespoke vessels require pricing on project basis. All prices are plus delivery. (Firearm options available where legal depending on country of buyer.)

USAGE GUIDELINES
All survival canoes and kayaks are short-range boats in practical terms simply due to human limitations. They can be used for longer journeys but only with planning. These types of journeys will involve frequent camps and stops, as well as the constant vigilance of being in water with possible floating zombie threats. Fighting zombies from a boat is challenging at best and flight is often the best policy. You are also vulnerable to armed human raiders and combat against such opponents is better handled ashore. Skirting the coast can be a useful tactic as you can monitor for any potential foraging locations.

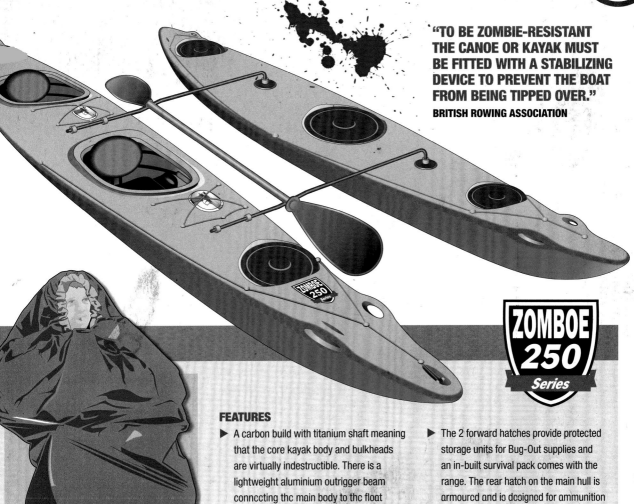

ZOMBOE 250 Series

IN-BUILT SURVIVAL BAG

Strong, lightweight survival bag designed to reduce rapid heat loss and the risk of hypothermia in emergency situations. It is made of heavy-duty polyethylene, is highly scratch resistant, and is coated in an anti-zombie chemical deterrent.

FEATURES

▶ A carbon build with titanium shaft meaning that the core kayak body and bulkheads are virtually indestructible. There is a lightweight aluminium outrigger beam connccting thc main body to thc float stabilizer (secondary hull).

▶ A specially designed seat and cockpit arrangement, with waterproof side arm pouch and reinforced hip and knee bracers – all designed for long-distance travel and use.

▶ Concealed front and rear flotation bags in both hulls, which are sculpted into the boat providing room for 6 watertight storage wells, plus an additional concealed unit by the side of the cockpit.

▶ All boats in the kayak range have a unique double-fin skeg underneath which further stabilises the boat and makes it easy to direct.

▶ The 3 wells on the main float include an in-built mini water purification unit and water-cooling storage unit.

▶ The 2 forward hatches provide protected storage units for Bug-Out supplies and an in-built survival pack comes with the range. The rear hatch on the main hull is armourcd and io dcoignod for ammunition and small firearms.

▶ The anti-zombie marine paint is designed to both camouflage the vessel when on the water and the manufacturers insist that the chemical composition of the paint repels zombies although this fact has not been verified by the Ministry of Zombies.

▶ Each boat in the Zomboe 150 and 250 series comes with 2 high-performance Seattle Sports carbon-fiber shaft battle kayak paddles. Unlike standard paddles, these are designed to stand up to the abuse of endless paddling and whacking the occasional zombie in the water. Durable, efficient and impact-resistant – it's no surprise that these paddles have twice been voted "Apocalypse Paddle of the Year" by *Survivor Weekly* magazine.

TRAVELING BY AIR

Escaping the zombies by air has long been the preserve of those rich enough to own personal jets or private light aircraft but things are changing. For the first time, there are airborne options for the average zombie prepper.

In general, zombies and air transport don't mix well at all. Consider Heathrow airport on a bank holiday when the schools are out and seemingly everyone is simultaneously trying to check their over-sized luggage in. Into this, hurl a zombie outbreak with a few hundred ghouls running wild and the result makes major airports one of the worst places to be during the zombie apocalypse. Equally, a zombie outbreak actually on board a plane will leave most survivors scratching their heads thinking, what the hell can you do in such a confined space? Well, in this section, we'll review air travel as an option in your Bug-Out Plans, and whilst it's true that you're unlikely to be able to pick up a cheap no-frills flight to safety in the sun, thanks to advances in technology, particularly in experimental ultra-light aircraft such as the Xtreme Survivor range from World Gyrocopters, air travel is now becoming a practical alternative.

BUGGING-OUT BY AIR

Most of those serious about their zombie apocalypse transportation will discount major airports and air travel from their Bug-Out Plans. However, as has been mentioned, there are still some useful options out there. It's worth remembering that most airborne Bug-Out Vehicles come with hefty price tags as well as sizeable training and maintenance costs.

The average zombie survivalist on a modest budget should certainly consider their airborne options. Gaining a pilot's licence, getting to know smaller local airports or exploring the potential of the new breed of gyrocopters are all reasonable tasks as you develop your Zombie Survival Plan. Carefully think through your Bug-Out Plans before you make any major commitments. For example, if you're planning a one-way trip to the wilderness with yourself, your family and Bug-Out Supplies, then investing in reasonable airborne transportation may be a viable option.

OPTION 1
SMALL RECREATIONAL AIRCRAFT

PROS
▶ According to the Light Aircraft Association, owning, maintaining and training on a smaller plane is no longer the preserve of the super-rich with options available for most budgets.
▶ There are over 50 commercial airports throughout the country, each with machines and training opportunities.
▶ The planes themselves require shorter runways than larger jets but can still evacuate a reasonable sized party and supplies.

CONS
▶ Although it is now cheaper, it's still a substantial cost – for example, $40,000 will get you a reasonable used plane but then you have all of the other costs...
▶ Ideally, you'd need to be very near your plane when the crisis hits. Even local airports are bound to become dicey once the zombies arrive.

OPTION 2
HELICOPTERS

PROS
▶ Shares many of the same benefits as smaller aircraft although lessons can still set you back hundreds of pounds per hour.
▶ Helicopters are far more flexible due to their unique vertical take-off and landing ability. It is therefore feasible for one or some of your party to guard the chopper when it is put down close to your home to pick up the rest of the survivors and supplies.

CONS
▶ Budget again – Bugging-Out by chopper won't be cheap unless you happen to chance upon a machine and a trained pilot who has nothing better to do.
▶ Most choppers are noisy and that's a big drawback as landing anywhere will attract every unsavory bandit in the local area, keen to get their grubby hands on your transport and supplies.

TRAVELING BY AIR
PERSONAL JET PACKS

Personal jet pack travel was the great hope of zombie survivalists in the 1960s with the early preppers dreaming of flying to safety at the press of a booster button. Survivors with a quality jet pack hoped that they could repeat their air escape multiple times, enabling them to use air hop across the rooftops, keeping well away from any zombies and the infected.

That was the dream but in reality personal jet or rocket-propelled transport has never lived up to its billing. It's dangerous, unreliable, and expensive. Not a good combination. There has been some useful work done around jet-propelled personal devices but much of it by unlicensed companies looking to cash in on the technology released by NASA in early 2001.

  More recently, the jet pack market has been flooded with rogue units, many of which are ineffective and even lethal. With little or no concern for user safety, using one of these cheaply made units is like strapping a leaky propane gas cylinder to your back then lighting it – not recommended.

OPTION 3
ULTRA-LIGHT AIRCRAFT

PROS

▶ Ultra-light aircraft like gyrocopters and microlights have never been more accessible. There are hundreds of clubs and courses throughout the country.
▶ Whilst specialist machines like the Xtreme Survivor 100Z range are expensive, you can get a decent second-hand machine for under $13,000.
▶ Many machines now have robust multi-fuel engines. You can't quite put anything in the tanks but fuel is certainly not such an issue for these aircraft.

CONS

▶ If you keep your aircraft in the garden or close to your home, it's a real challenge to keep things quiet from neighbors. Remember that friendly person down the road could turn into a desperate knife-wielding lunatic demanding that you take them with you.
▶ Most machines have limited space for people and supplies, with strict weight limitations.

OPTION 4
HOT-AIR BALLOONS AND BLIMPS

PROS

▶ Massive advances have been made in this field of air transport in recent years, with successful circumnavigations and altitude challenges.
▶ Many options, particularly hot-air or helium balloons are virtually silent so why not combine your desperate Bug-Out escape with some delightful views of the burning remains of civilization. Ensure that you pack a picnic basket.

CONS

▶ Hard to find, unreliable and requiring substantial ground support means that currently hot-air balloons and blimps are the stuff of fantasy for serious zombie survivalists.
▶ The uncontrollable nature of hot-air balloons could see you coming down in a field of zombies. Blimps are better equipped but equally impractical for all but a few qualified experts.

TRAVELING BY AIR

AIRPORTS AND ZOMBIES

For many, the idea of flying to some safe zone is the perfect escape route from a zombie apocalypse but in reality, unless you have a private plane on a guarded private air strip, the chances are if you try to make it to the nearest airport, you'll either be caught by a deadly rush of survivors, all clambering to get on flights which have long-since been canceled, or you'll end up stuck in bumper to bumper traffic miles from the terminal. Basically, major airports are no-go areas once the dead show up.

In 2016, the Civil Aviation Authority produced a detailed assessment of the resilience of the country's airports and air travel infrastructure. The document listed "viral incident" – a codeword for zombie outbreak often used in official documentation – as the second most imminent threat to the air travel network. There is no doubt that our brave armed response units will put up a good fight against the infected but the report left zombie preppers in no doubt – "The airport network is extremely vulnerable to any viral incidents, particularly where such incidents involve violent and cannibalistic symptoms." Civil Aviation Authority Preparedness Report, March 2016. Bureaucratic jargon which roughly translates as if we have a major zombie outbreak at an airport, jumbo jet will mean jumbo human buffet for the dead.

▶ ZOMBIES ON A PLANE

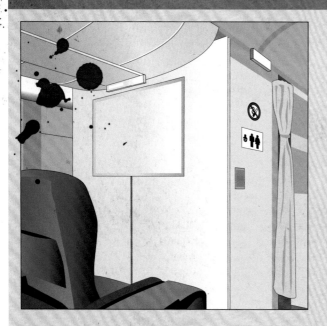

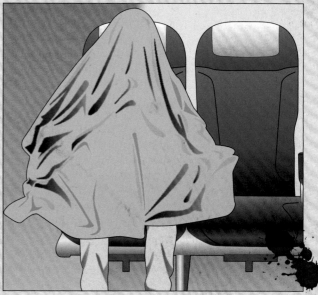

STEP 1
ASSESS THE RISK

Once you're aware of the warning signs, keep an eye out for those with flu-like symptoms. Always select a seat close to the front or back of the plane, if possible close to the bathroom and kitchen area. Report any symptoms to staff as soon as possible. All air crew and support staff are trained to spot symptoms of the zombic condition.

STEP 2
MAKE YOUR MOVE

If the worst happens and you see someone "on the turn," it is vital you make your move quickly. Quietly, get as far away as you can – the best location is towards the front of the plane. With very few items available on board as weapons, grab any sweaters or coats you can to at least provide some protection. Blankets can also be used to hurl over infected individuals.

TRAVELING BY AIR
AIR TRAVEL Q&A

In 2017, the Ministry of Zombies sponsored a series of radio helpline slots on national radio as part of its "Zombie Defense in the Community" program. One show focused exclusively on air travel and the questions and answers below may help illuminate some of the key challenges and misunderstandings about Bugging-Out by air.

IF I ALREADY HAVE A TICKET AND GET TO THE AIRPORT, WILL THE AIRLINE HONOR MY TICKET?

It is unlikely that you'll be able to get in the door at the airport. Expect canceled flights, heaving crowds and riots. The fact that you have a ticket to somewhere won't make that much difference.

WILL A ZOMBIE APOCALYPSE AFFECT THE AMOUNT OF LUGGAGE I CAN TAKE ON BOARD? I FEEL THAT 50 LBS IS TOO RESTRICTIVE.

Are you serious? We're talking about getting on alive not whether you can afford to take your cricket whites on a summer holiday. You really should read up on the impact of a major zombie outbreak!

WILL I BE ABLE TO USE AIR MILES TO FUND MY ESCAPE BY AIR?

Your air miles are unlikely to buy you an escape route. You may as well change your name to "Cheap Meat Snack" as far as the zombies are concerned. Can we get rid of this caller?

And so, like a poorly thought through forum discussion on Reddit, the phone-in slot descended into chaos. Clearly, the general public weren't ready for an open discussion on the threat posed by the walking dead.

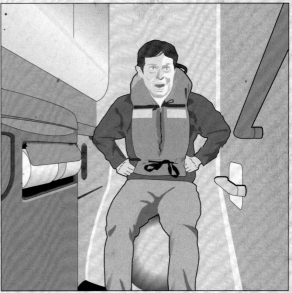

STEP 3
CONTAINMENT

Join any like-minded survivors in containing the infected area. Barricade off a section of the plane using items such as luggage or catering carts. You'll need to be ruthless as there will doubtless be some living trapped outside but do your best to help them. Let the pilot team, who will be securely sealed off in the front, deal with getting the aircraft to safety.

STEP 4
CONTAINMENT FAILURE

If your containment fails, grab water, food, and any uninflated lifejackets and lock yourself in one of the toilets. You can assume the pilots are still safely locked in the cockpit but if the plane starts to behave erratically and you fear a crash landing, inflate the life jackets around you to create a protective cocoon... It's your best chance of surviving.

TRAVELING BY AIR

BUGGING-OUT BY GYROCOPTER

So you've decided that the gyrocopter is the right option for Bugging-Out – there is certainly plenty of choice out there on the market, including the 100Z range profiled here – but before you buy a leather flying jacket and consider which shades to wear to get that ultimate pilot look, there are some things to consider – in addition, of course, to the major decision about what machine to buy.

▶ Get all the training and practice you can before Z-Day arrives. Get qualified with the right pilot's licence then get plenty of hours in the air. The more skilled a pilot you are, the better the chances that you will reach your Bug-Out Location.

▶ Plan your Bug-Out Route carefully; assume that any GPS technology will be down. Learn to navigate by landmarks. One of the simplest ways is to use our motorways to guide you. If you can, complete an entire practice run. Try starting at night if you are experienced enough.

▶ Keep your machine as discreetly as possible. Some preppers buy two machines, keeping one at the airfield, and one hidden nearer to their home. Not everyone has that kind of budget but ensure that your machine is hidden and accessible in a crisis. The ideal set up would include a runway area close to home, even if it's just a field at the end of the garden.

▶ Watch the weight on your machine. Get the balance of supplies right as an over-weight gyrocopter could get you killed. Know the tolerances of your plane and be cautious about who is coming with you. If you have room for 1 plus your Bug-Out Supplies then don't be tempted to squeeze another desperate survivor on board if you only have a 2-seater.

▶ Scout your long-term Bug-Out Location carefully. If possible, hide extra fuel and supplies on site. Always have a back up location and check out potential stop off points if it's going to be a longer journey.

TRAVELING BY AIR
LANDING GUIDELINES

Most of your flight training will take place on a structured flight program and your tutors may or may not be aware of your zombie Bug-Out Plans. Much of what you learn will be relevant but you should also be aware of the particular challenges a zombie apocalypse will bring. Remember, if you don't know an area always assume it is hostile. One drawback of a gyrocopter is that below a certain height, the noise can attract unwanted attention from both the living and the dead.

FOUR STEP PROCESS FOR LANDING

1 Complete an eyeball and sensor scan of the area. Check out any principle landmarks and identify a safe landing zone.
2 Drop a synthetic meat bomb a few miles away to draw off any zombie hordes in the area.
3 Pop a smoke bomb down at a similar location, it can distract hostile bandits into thinking survivors are in that location.
4 Once on the ground, complete a further eye ball and sensor scan. Always be ready to get out of Dodge as soon as possible if required.

XTREME SURVIVOR 100Z GYROCOPTER

What if there was a relatively cheap experimental flying machine available? What if it needed only very basic training and a bit of open space to take off? Well, the Xtreme Survivor range from World Gyrocopters has been developed just to fill this niche in the zombie survival market for an affordable and practical airborne long-range Bug-Out Vehicle.

XTREME SURVIVOR 100Z GYROCOPTER

World Gyrocopters, Lydd Airport, Kent

LOCATION

Over 100 models sold, so all over the world. Showroom in Lydd, Kent.

PURPOSE

A high-performance ultra-light aircraft designed especially for post-apocalyptic use as a Bug-Out Vehicle.

CREW

Available in solo, twin-seater or quad-seat configurations.

TECHNICAL SPECIFICATIONS

Air framework in high-grade stainless steel, electro "walking dead" polished. Tinted zombie-proof plexiglass windscreens, front and side. All aluminium welded 30 gallon fuel cell. Apocalypse IP 360 Engine, 225 hp with mounted fuel pump and super-filters. Military-grade main landing gear. High-performance rotor system with 80 inch carbon fiber blades.

ARMAMENTS

Standard model is unarmed but has fixing points for a door-mounted machine gun and under-carriage anti-zombie chaff-missile pods as well as a host of other features to help the pilot combat the undead, such as the refrigerated "meat bomb," which drops hunks of synthetic human flesh designed to attract zombies to a particular location, and the revolutionary "Cool Body Sensor" system, which uses a special form of infrared heat sensing camera to detect movement and the lower body temperature of a zombie.

USAGE GUIDELINES

Airborne Bugging-Out is the dream of many zombie preppers and this range of British-made gyrocopters makes it possible. The 2-seater version needs a maximum of 300 feet for take-off but only 60 feet for landing and with a maximum range of 400 miles on the standard version, once you are prepped with your vehicle, start planning your perfect Bug-Out Location. Preppers tend to recommend the twin-seater version as it has significantly more stowage space.

RANGE

With the extended 30 gallon fuel tank plus additional apocalypse-grade drop tank of 15 gallons, the twin-seat 100Z range can comfortably cover up to 400 miles fully loaded at an average cruise speed of around 80 mph at 10,000 feet.

BUDGET

Base model Xtreme Survivor 100Z Gyrocopter is $58,000 plus transportation. Comes with anti-zombie features as standard. The Xtreme Survivor 200Z Gyrocopter is the 4-seater version and is custom built to order – most units costing around $100,000.

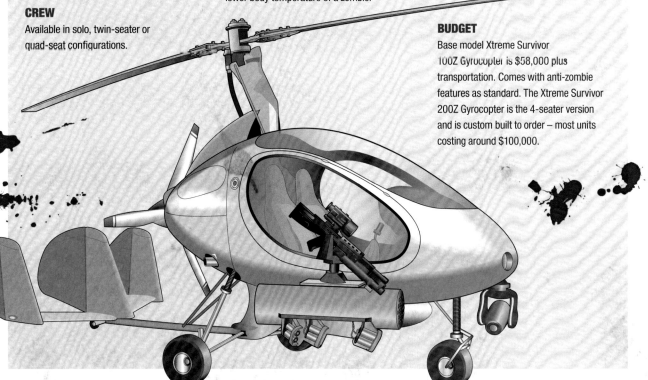

GLOSSARY

Ambush To attack by surprise from a hiding place.

Apocalypse The complete final destruction of the world.

Cannibal   Animals that eat their own kind

Crossbow Bows mounted across wooden blocks.

Forage To hunt or search for something.

Ghoul A zombie or evil creature.

Infrared Light waves that are outside of the visible part of the light range at the red end, which we can see.

Maneuver A movement or series of moves requiring skill and care.

Navigation The act of guiding a vehicle, ship, or aircraft.

Pannier A basket or bag carried on a bicycle or beast of burden.

Survivalist A person who practices survival skills and tries to ensure their own survival.

FOR FURTHER READING

Austin, John. *So Now You're a Zombie: A Handbook for the Newly Undead.* Chicago: Chicago Review Press, 2010.

Brooks, Max. *The Zombie Survival Guide: Complete Protection from the Living Dead.* New York: Crown Archetype, 2003.

Brooks, Max. *World War Z: An Oral History of the Zombie War.* New York: Crown Archetype, 2007.

Luckhurst, Roger. *Zombies: A Cultural History.* London: Reaktion Books, 2015.

Ma, Roger. *The Zombie Combat Manual: A Guide to Fighting the Living Dead.* London: Penguin Publishing Group, 2010.

FOR MORE INFORMATION

https://www.cdc.gov/phpr/zombie/index.htm

https://www.cnn.com/2014/05/16/politics/pentagon-zombie-apocalypse/index.html

https://www.forbes.com/sites/kevinmurnane/2017/01/08/guess-how-many-people-will-survive-a-zombie-apocalypse/#5801616c5e40

https://www.natgeokids.com/uk/discover/science/general-science/zombie-apocalypse-survival/

https://www.rei.com/blog/social/infographic-13-essential-tools-for-surviving-a-zombie-outbreak

INDEX